To
THomAS
THANKS For
VISITINH —
US
Ziegler
2017

ISBN: 10:0-9908554-8-1
ISBN: 13:978-0-9908554-8-4
Library of Congress Control Number: 2011919793
CreateSpace Independent Publishing Platform

Printed in the United States of America

Designed by Essie Dubé

Bailey Brook Farm

A Memoir

Based on Transcripts From
The Bill Kelly Radio Show

William A. Kelly

Acknowledgements

I dedicate this book to Timothy E. Murphy, who bet on a long shot and apparently won! I thank God for sending me my son, William Kelly Jr. and my daughter, Mary Madeline. I thank Him for providing me with a wife, Kelly Kelly (yes, that's her name), who has been my partner in life in every way. Many thanks to my editor and designer, Essie Dubé, for rescuing this work and connecting the chapters with her silver thread of coherence. Finally, and most importantly, I thank God for all the adversity, without which I would never have been able to enjoy and appreciate this moment so much. The unburdening is now complete.

❧ CONTENTS ❧

CHAPTER ONE
Early Recollections   1

CHAPTER TWO
Bailey Brook Farm   5

CHAPTER THREE
Gathering Eggs 13

CHAPTER FOUR
Gramp's Values 17

CHAPTER FIVE
Kelly Feeling Bad 25

CHAPTER SIX
Mom Said It 29

CHAPTER SEVEN
Mr. Pick 35

CHAPTER EIGHT
My Irish Mom 39

CHAPTER NINE
The Value of a Paper Route 43

CHAPTER TEN
Paper Route People 49

CHAPTER ELEVEN
The Boy Scout Code 53

Contents

CHAPTER TWELVE
The Dream of Vaudeville 59

CHAPTER THIRTEEN
What It Means to be Irish 63

CHAPTER FOURTEEN
A Moral Compass 67

CHAPTER FIFTEEN
My Prayer in the Woods 73

CHAPTER SIXTEEN
The Proper Use of Power 77

CHAPTER SEVENTEEN
Tim Murphy, Part One 81

CHAPTER EIGHTEEN
Tim Murphy, Part Two 85

CHAPTER NINETEEN
William Kelly Jr. 93

CHAPTER TWENTY
Cookies 95

CHAPTER TWENTY-ONE
In My Room 97

CHAPTER TWENTY-TWO
School Days Then and Now 101

CHAPTER TWENTY-THREE
How to Tell You Are in a Family 103

Contents

CHAPTER TWENTY-FOUR
School Clothes 107

CHAPTER TWENTY-FIVE
Getting A Break 111

CHAPTER TWENTY-SIX
What We Did Not Have 119

CHAPTER TWENTY-SEVEN
The Farm in Spring 125

CHAPTER TWENTY-EIGHT
Gertrude T. Kelly 129

CHAPTER TWENTY-NINE
The Day I Lived 137

Prologue

The following pages contain excerpts from my Saturday-morning radio show on WRKO in Boston. We have woven these edited transcripts into "chapters" of my life at Bailey Brook Farm. Over the years, audience reaction to my stories of growing up on the farm has been incredible. That reaction was the impetus for the book you are about to read. It is my gift not only to my listeners, but also to any reader along the way who yearns for "the good old days."

You will find some repetition, some "story-telling" liberties and, I hope, a great deal of entertaining reading within its pages. I thank the 50,000 or so listeners who have called during the past seven years and I look forward to hearing from many thousands more in the years to come. Enjoy the book and should you feel the need to call the radio show, you know where I am!

CHAPTER ONE
Early Recollections

I awoke three years ago on a cold January morning, turned to the large window and gazed out over the ocean. The digital thermometer read minus 8 degrees outdoors and 72 degrees indoors. I glanced behind me and there, in the king-sized bed, was my 5-year-old son, William Kelly Jr., fast asleep. The landscape was barely visible, as it was 5:45 a.m. and the sun had not yet risen.

My mind flashed back to my 5-year-old self on Bailey Brook Farm in the winter. With the temperature rapidly approaching 8 degrees below zero, I had to get up quite early with my grandfather, Tim Murphy. All of the outdoor pipes were frozen, so we had to carry the water in pails down to the hen coops. That meant opening the bulkhead door that led to the basement, then filling buckets with water and walking them down to the coops. At age 5, I used a rusty old tin beach bucket and was happy to do my part to assist.

I remember standing in the hen coop one frigid morning. The air was thick in this dimly lighted space and the close odor was made almost palpable by the dangerous cold. After we had dropped the food and water, the hens scampered over to the troughs to eat and drink. While they were busy, Gramp and I went to the roosts to gather eggs.

Thirty years earlier, he had been a wealthy industrialist in Providence. His Florentine bride, Gertrude Notini, was the most beautiful young woman in Cranston and she pursued Gramp with a skillful balance of zeal and reserve, so he would always feel he was the pursuer. He proposed and they married.

Eight children later, they were living happily in the Eden Park section of Cranston, in one of a pair of homes my grandfather built. A three-floor Victorian faced its twin, which Gramp gave to his in-laws, my great-grandfather Notini and his wife, Emma, who looked after the children as they helped my grandmother.

Providence was one big jewelry factory, a bright star and the world leader in production. One could drive through the jewelry district at 3 a.m. and find factory windows glowing. In the blink of an eye, however, it all went dark and disappeared. One of the first casualties of the Great Depression, following the stock market itself, was the jewelry industry.

Well, there we both stood, in a quiet hen coop on a morning of minus-8-degree weather, 25 years after the crash. I wonder if Gramp had ever thought about how he went from being the toast of Cranston to gathering eggs in that coop. He was never bitter and rarely talked about his losses. From 1950 to 1975, he stayed focused on the task at hand, helping to raise us all and making sure we made it out into the world with skills we could harness for success. But I know it must have been a long, tough trip from the top of the world to the inside of a hen coop, there with his 5-year-old buddy on that freezing morning.

I have been all over the world and have met many famous, wonderful people. I have fallen, but unlike Gramp, I was able to recover. After writing this book, I now realize why. It was Gramp's example, wisdom and teachings that allowed me to survive and then thrive.

What Gramp did for me was to place in my heart and soul a special device that would be triggered if I ever reached a low point at which I might have given up. It was designed to activate if I were ever in danger of total failure, to protect me from losing all and falling over a cliff from which there might have been no return. He instilled in me an ideal that encouraged me to overcome many difficulties. In the end, I was able to arrive at a good place, a place from which I could begin the process again with my *own* 5-year-old son.

I don't know which section of Heaven you occupy, Gramp, but wherever you are, I'm sure they are enjoying your company and laughing at your jokes about the old Irish living on Smith Hill. I miss you today as much as ever, perhaps more, because I have so much to share with you and there is so much catching up to do. I'll see you on the other side some day. I will always love you.

Your grandson,
"Murph"

CHAPTER TWO

Bailey Brook Farm

At times, I still find it difficult to believe there once was a Bailey Brook Farm where I grew up. It seems so out of sync with what's happening nowadays. Rest assured, there *was* such a farm. People under the age of 45 might think it is all just a fable. It is not. They might find it surprising we had a sock bag, a rag bag and a single bathroom for 10 people: five of us kids, two foster brothers, John and Richie, our two parents and, of course, Gramp. We had our own version of The Peaceable Kingdom. Chickens and dogs slept in a pile with the cats.

We also had a peddler named Mr. Pick, a bread man, a milkman and the Fuller Brush man. The Carters drove to our farm to buy eggs and Mr. Silveria delivered sacks of chicken feed from the Purina store each week. In March, he brought cardboard boxes filled with tiny baby chicks. We would put them under small, heated tents in the brooder coop and carefully watch over them, making sure their little troughs were always filled with grain and water.

In the spring, Uncle Tom came with his shotgun to kill the chicken hawks, which was probably illegal. Skunks, foxes and weasels were the main predators vying for a meal of fresh eggs or chicken breast. Lightning storms ruined our egg harvest and hurricanes threatened our hen coops.

My folks had three jobs collectively. We had one car and lived almost a mile from the main road. The rocky, dirt lane leading up to our home was a daily adventure and it wasn't long before we knew every crook, rock and bump in the lane by heart.

We walked to school in winter, spring, summer and fall. It was exactly a mile and a half, so it wasn't terrible. I cannot figure out why we didn't ride our bicycles. We were out the door by 7:30 a.m. and back home by 3:30 p.m.. There were no cell phones, beepers or text messages. Life then was simple. Unplugged. We left for school, the school I loved. At the end of our school day, we headed home to play and run. I loved my farm. I loved all of my schools and all of my teachers.

There was one teacher, Mr. Esperanto, who had an unusual way of greeting kids within striking distance of him in the hall. He would punch them in the shoulder and then adjust his college ring, so the next kid he punched got hit in the arm with the ring just right. Obviously, kids weren't anxious to walk near Mr. Esperanto. Can you imagine what would happen nowadays if a teacher did that? He would probably be in jail.

We carried our lunch to school, as there was no cafeteria. After eating lunch, we headed out for an hour of recess, running around at top speed, raising Cain, having fun and forming gangs. Gangs back then were a little bit different than today's gangs. Members of our gang were the guys we hung around with at recess and with whom we played football.

That is a bygone era for sure. Now everything's expensive, everything's by appointment and everything is pre-planned. Kids are being driven to soccer matches, lacrosse games, swimming practice and after-school clubs. It has all changed. Is it change for the better? I think the new political correctness has caused a lot of frustration, and the federal school programs seem to have left millions of children behind. Why are third-graders being taught to subtract two numbers using six steps (Common Core), when we did the same problem using only two steps. The trend seems to be more toward complicating life than simplifying it for the kids.

There are some positive things happening, however. My wife, Kelly, and I went to our daughter's school recently on parents' night and it was jam-packed, standing room only. We had to sign in and wait in line to meet the teachers. They know every student and we receive regular emails about the progress of both of our children.

My son is in a charter school. From what I can gather, a charter school nowadays means a school just like the one I attended in 1958. Back then we just called it "school." There were very few students per teacher, a high tracking ratio, a high success rate and a lot of quality time. Parents cared and teachers went the extra mile. I could be wrong about that definition, and I'm sure someone will correct me if I am, but to me a charter school is exactly like the Howland School I attended in the New England countryside.

Our principal was Mrs. Caroll and our janitor was Uncle Jessie. They pretty much ran the school. Mrs. Caroll would look right at you and make you stick out your tongue. If it was black, you were lying, and that was that. Since the color of your tongue determined your fate, we obviously did not eat too much licorice. Uncle Jessie had both a secret red powder that would eradicate "throw-up" and a cloth bin with wheels for the trash. When someone got sick at school, Uncle Jessie came with the powder and swept away the mess, as if it had never happened.

My family was pro-teacher. If something was wrong on my report card, I, and not the teacher, had to pay the price. We had mid-term reports back then. If I came home with a yellow slip for my mid-terms, it wasn't going to be a happy weekend. We used to call them "deficiencies" and hoped we wouldn't get any. If I did something great, on the other hand, I received a commendation for that mid-term and couldn't wait to bring it home. Such was life back then.

To me, school was like a daily Broadway play. No, I take that back. It was like six to eight Broadway plays each day. To others, these were called "classes." I felt almost as if my teachers were there to entertain me and teach me. It was so exciting and so new each time I went to school. I could always sense a focus upon my well-being by each of my teachers.

When I was in fifth grade, I would wake up in the morning and go to my older brother Michael's closet after he left for school, steal one of his shirts and bring it down to the dining room. The ironing board was usually set up, so I'd iron the shirt and my khakis too, if they needed it. From junior high on, I bought my own shoes and wore penny loafers when I could afford to. When I reached high school, there were lunches I could buy for a quarter. Believe it or not, lunches were terrific back then. I understand much of what the kids are served now is thrown away, because it just isn't appetizing to them. Every bit of my high school lunches was eaten.

I think the most impressive aspect of my schooling was the teachers. I respected them so much because they held the keys to our future and they made learning really enjoyable. This was particularly true of our teachers in history and English. They made things so much fun. While learning about various authors, I would get hooked on one and read everything he or she had written. At the end of grade school, I got into the *Hardy Boys* series and read all 66 books. They were hardbound books that sold for 99 cents each. Since they were written in the '30s, by 1963 they were dated, but they were fun to read and they were enjoyable. In high school, I got into Hemingway, Faulkner, and Sir Arthur Conan Doyle's *Sherlock Holmes* stories. Those were incredible. Our life was structured around fantasy, respect for teachers and others in authority, and the survival of a large, Irish family. It was the American way.

The importance of the holidays back then impressed me most. We had so many people come to see us at home. For our part, we visited friends regularly and rotated where we would spend certain holidays, especially Thanksgiving and Christmas. Every year, we'd have a summer picnic down by the beach or in a park near Cranston. There would be close to 80 people — 22 cousins, 20 aunts, 20 uncles and more. We would even invite other friends of the family, all great people. Everyone would come. Those were the days. Those were most *definitely* the days. But these are the days, too, because we're living longer and enjoying it more.

So now we confront part of the challenge: Can we reconcile the America of my youth with the America of today? And is it still America? Does it feel okay to let people know how proud we are of the United States of America, of what we do here, the potential we have and the things we accomplish? For example, a heart attack used to be a death sentence, but today it is just a blip on the screen.

A heart attack means you will have all these procedures and help in creating a new diet. The doctors are going to give you life-saving drugs and an opportunity to live. So it's sort of a wake-up call now, whereas it used to be a death sentence. I believe the survival rate for cancer is steadily increasing as we get closer to finding a cure. Today, many people live with diseases that once were considered life-threatening.

We never thought of wearing a safety belt in the car when I was young. We rode in the back seat of a '57 Chevy and there was a cable across it. Does anyone know what the purpose of that cable was, except to pull on it and bug the living daylights out of your parents? Basically, our pulling on the cable would get the driver all upset. The driver was usually my father. He'd talk a lot but would never yell. My mother, however, could reach every corner of that '57 Chevy with the back of her hand, and she had a formidable backhand. So we knew if we were going to pull on the cable, we had better duck, because Mom would be trying to whack us.

Mom had a piece of tissue, and no matter what happened on the way to church, she could fix it with that tissue. She would look us up and down in the car and then she'd lick the tissue and rub a shirt or face, adjust the hair with her fingernails, look us over again, and move on to the next child.

Mom could get us all shined up by the time we got to Mass, which was not a long ride from our farm. A great Mass to me is under 40 minutes. You're out of there with a good sermon and it's nice and compact. Back then it was probably an hour.

Fifty-five minutes was the "over-under," but if you wanted to wait until 11 a.m. at St. Mary's, you could attend the High Mass. So you paid the price for the extra sleep and the luxury of the late Mass. That meant two priests. It also meant that everything was in Latin, from start to finish, with hymns, bells and incense. So that was the High Mass and that was the reward for sleeping in late on Sunday. I got to be closer to God for an hour and 40 minutes as a result of my lax sleeping habits, according to Mom.

St. Mary's is on the corner of Memorial Boulevard and Spring Street in Newport, Rhode Island. It's the church in which John F. Kennedy and Jacqueline Bouvier became man and wife. When we got out of High Mass, Mr. Hussy would be there with his old Chevy van full of newspapers. They were a quarter each. I would buy a *Boston Globe,* a *Boston Herald* and a *Providence Journal,* bring them home and read for about an hour. I really liked the sports and editorial sections, and reading about the thoughts of different people all over America. Don't ask me why they were so appealing, but that's what I was into in fourth grade. In the mid-afternoon we'd watch either a football or baseball game. In the early evening, it was dinnertime, and we would sit down to a roast beef dinner. That was our Sunday, every Sunday.

I also enjoyed reading the *TV Guide.* On our television we had three channels: CBS, NBC, and a brand new network, ABC. PBS was just getting started. I would plan out my television week, starting with *Bonanza* and *Hopalong Cassidy* on Saturday. I would circle all the programs in the *TV Guide* that we kids wanted to watch, knowing that at 6:30 p.m. it was going to be *The Huntley-Brinkley Report,* no matter what I had circled. If we wanted to watch it, great. If we didn't, we were welcome to find something else to do.

I remember getting ready for school in the morning, and Gramp would be watching Dave Garroway on the original *Today* show. He also watched *The Tonight Show* every night, from its first day on television until the day he entered the nursing home. The first time Gramp missed it was a January night in 1982. I'm sure he had a record going for consecutive shows viewed. Carson ended at 1 a.m.. Gramp went to bed right after that and got up around 10 each morning.

It was an interesting life at Bailey Brook Farm. The way we lived, the things we did, the things we saw and the people who came in and out of our lives were all very interesting and all very sweet. I don't know how those times could ever be replicated or reclaimed. Maybe Heaven is going back to the loveliest time you experienced as a child and reliving it over and over again. It would certainly feel like Heaven to me if someday someone said, "That's what it is, Bill, and we'll see you there."

CHAPTER THREE
Delivering Eggs

G rowing up seems now to be a distant dream to me. In it, I'm transported back to my large immediate and extended family—my grandfather, my folks, my brothers and sisters and my dog, Minnie. Looking back on my life, the varied experiences we had seem as if they took place in a foreign land or on another planet. Things are so complex these days.

During the holiday season, and generally on Christmas Eve, Gramp would hand me an envelope. When I was nine years old, there would be $2 in that envelope. By the time I was entering college, the Christmas envelope had $25 in it. How I waited for that envelope each year! Gramp and I would sit at the table late at night. As he handed it to me, he would ask me to review the past year and preview the year ahead. What were my goals? What was I thinking? Where was I headed?

Eventually, I decided I wanted to learn to use computers for flight simulation. That was in 1974 and the Air Force had agreed to send me away to school. At the time, the thought of going away to school was insufferable to me. It meant I was heading out. The team consisting of me and my grandfather, Tim Murphy, would be broken up. And what a team it was! We were together for more than 22 years. Kelly and Murphy, I guess you could call it. When I was a baby, I slept in a room with Gramp. As I grew, I moved upstairs with the other six kids. We were piled up there, one on top of the other, fighting for survival. Life on a farm in a large family.

When I was 3 or 4 years old, I remember waking up and getting myself down to the kitchen by 9 a.m., so I could watch Gramp make oatmeal. Through the years we had many long talks over that oatmeal. He would have a cup of Maxwell House coffee with PET evaporated milk in the can, one spoonful of sugar and a piece of toast. Once in a while, my dog Minnie would sit near the table, looking up at us. Gramp would dip his toast in coffee and give her a piece. Minnie was a small, black mongrel and was probably the smartest animal I have ever known.

After breakfast, Gramp would sit me on the table, so he could tie my shoes, put on my coat and zip me up. Then off we would go. In the winter, I added my mittens and hat as he and I walked out the door and went down to take care of the chickens. Gramp had a wire basket that would hold about 10 dozen eggs. He fed the chickens with Purina pellets from a cloth sack, and we walked back and forth, bringing buckets of water to put in the troughs. Then, while the chickens were eating, he collected their eggs to store in our stone-walled cellar. Our house was built around 1880. The furnace was quite old, but there was a root cellar in the basement. We stored all the eggs there until Wednesday night, at which time we would candle them.

How does one candle an egg? Well, it's pretty simple. First you hold the egg up to the light, to make sure there's not a baby chick inside. If there is, you put the egg aside and if there isn't, it goes in the egg carton. After sorting the eggs, we brought them down to a place near the beach called the County Food Mart. My mother generally drove us there in our gray '55 Chevy station wagon with the fins. We would bring the eggs in and give them to Mr. Sanchez, the owner of the food mart, who would give us cash and a store credit to do some shopping. If I was lucky, I would get some candy. The butcher at the food mart was named Tony. Tony the butcher would prepare the roasts to order, while Mom entertained him with stories about all kinds of things that were happening on the farm.

The first stop after County Food Mart was the Industrial National Bank. In later years, Industrial National Bank became Fleet Bank, then Bank of America. My grandfather would make a deposit with his bank passbook, then come out of the bank with money for my mother. He would first hand it to me as a joke and say, "Here, give this to your mother." That money helped her to support the house. We had food, Gramp had some savings and Mom had extra money. When Gramp began receiving Social Security, he gave Mom half of it. He lived with us, and he helped raise us. There is no doubt he raised *me*. Gramp contributed to the household until he left in the ambulance for the nursing home, some 30 years later.

We had dogs. We had cats. We had food. We had bicycles. We had hand-me-down shoes. And we had the inevitable sock bag. Whenever someone did a wash and the socks didn't match up, he or she would put the odd socks in a bag. Just imagine this. Seven kids, and every month or so we would go through the sock bag and match up the stray pairs. We also had a rag bag of old sheets, towels and cloths we used for all sorts of things. That is how we lived.

We seven children had paper routes, starting at age 8 or 9. On those routes, we got to know people and were able to work and produce. By doing that, we learned things.

Was it a perfect life? No, it was not. We had our problems. Did we get through them unscathed? For the most part, we did. But there are a lot of nicks on my soul that I know love and prayer will help heal. That is the reason my religion assumes such an important role in my life. It has given me an open invitation for forgiveness and renewal.

My childhood is now a distant dream, alive with fields, sunny days, winter snow drifts, playtime and family dinners. Did all that happen or did I just conjure it up to counterbalance a reality so daunting that I sometimes wonder if I'm up to this. Are *we* up to this? Do you know what? I believe deep in my heart that we *are* up to it and we will prevail.

CHAPTER FOUR

Gramp's Values

The more things change, the more they remain the same. One Thanksgiving, when I was about 7, Uncle Earl came over to the house. We had just purchased a brand new, 25-inch Zenith television. It was huge, weighing about 200 pounds, and when you turned it on, you could hear the whine while all the tubes warmed up. Then, all of a sudden, *boom*! And there was the picture. Back then, everyone was talking about the size of their televisions. It was like talking about the size of your engine. Actually, things haven't changed very much at all. At the Kelly Financial offices, we installed a new 58-inch plasma screen for clients to view their portfolios. Needless to say, they are all impressed with it.

About a month ago, I was reading an article about a 6-year-old boy in Boston. He got off the school bus and saw a little girl about the same age who seemed to be lost in a giant rain storm. He sat with her and protected her until a policeman came by to help her get home. That little boy was featured in the *Boston Globe* with the girl he had saved. It's so comforting to know there is still heroism in the world, even at the tender age of 6.

People worry about ending their lives in nursing homes. My grandfather, Tim Murphy, felt the same way. Gramp was probably the strongest man I ever knew and there wasn't much he couldn't do. Over the years he stood up to a lot, and he made it to the finish line with his head up.

As I said earlier, Gramp had a wonderful life until the crash of 1932, when his whole world suddenly changed. He was a wealthy industrialist and owned several six-family homes in Providence. He had a beautiful residence in a very nice section of Cranston, and his family had the best of everything. I have seen the census patterns and the forms they signed to attest to it. They had the nicest pianos and wonderful clothing. Then it was suddenly all gone.

Providence was the jewelry capital of the world. There were many factories for jewelry and silver place settings. My grandfather had a factory in which they enameled emblems for REO Motor Car Company. For the VFW, the Army and the Navy, they enameled emblems and buttons for uniforms.

In 1927, there were signs on the horizon that didn't bode well for anyone who owned a jewelry factory in Providence. As the financial markets collapsed in the late '20s and early '30s, Gramp didn't know what he was heading into. At first the darkness was on the horizon and then, like a tidal wave, it was at his front door.

He had to face that with eight children, no money and all of his houses going into foreclosure because no one could pay the rent. Even if he had evicted the tenants, he couldn't have found other tenants who had any money. Providence looked like a prison camp or a scene out of a Dickens movie, with people sitting on their front stoops all day. Nobody could find work. Why was Providence hit so hard? Middle-class people stopped buying jewelry. You couldn't eat jewelry. The collapse of the economy delivered a double hit, both for Providence and for Gramp.

So what did he do? Did he become paralyzed with despair? No, he went out and painted. He painted for the Works Progress Administration. In those days, they had to divide the family up. Aunts, uncles and cousins would take in children while the head of the household tried to earn enough money to pay for their food. New clothing was unheard of. Clothing was passed down from child to child.

Gramp got on his feet again through hard work, and was eventually able to help my parents buy Bailey Brook Farm. At the time, we were living in a project. There's nothing else you could call it. Gramp had saved up about $4,000, which was an unheard of sum back then. He used it as a down payment on the 27-acre farm for my parents. Gramp decided he was going to stay with us, and together they would pay the mortgage. Dad was a fireman and Mom was a telephone operator. I think both of those terms are improper or antiquated now, but that's what they called themselves and that's how we got our start, on a farm about a mile from the beach.

Everyone had to work. I always wondered if Gramp was bitter about all he had lost in his life. He was a perfectionist. He did the daily routine and he cared for us, but I think it may have been a difficult adjustment. Gramp had gone from being a pillar of Providence industry in 1932 to living in a farmhouse in 1952 with nine other people, all sharing one bathroom. He didn't seem to have a lot of regrets, and he certainly had a lot to teach us.

So what were the values my grandfather taught me? There were many. Respect for proper diction was one. When we got home from school, he would ask us grandkids about the words we had learned, and he would stress the importance of diction. "Good diction begins with the teeth, tongue and lips." I can still see him standing right there, saying it. If I had the vocal quality of some other people in radio, I think I'd be a billionaire. I am not on the radio because of my vocal talent and I don't have a show because I'm the sharpest person in radio. I'm here because I love what I'm doing, and apparently people like listening. That's the extent of it. But good diction was important to Gramp, and it has helped me to this day.

Respect for teachers was paramount in our house. If a note came home from school, it was a big event. It didn't generally bode well for us if the note said we weren't doing what we were supposed to be doing. If I was the culprit, there was definitely a meeting after dinner with a committee comprised of Mom and Gramp, or Mom and Dad. They sided with the school almost 100 percent of the time. They didn't call the school and threaten to sue the teacher. They called the school and said, "It's taken care of. If it happens again, please let us know."

Respect for law and order, paying taxes and being a good citizen were all taught to us at an early age. Another value we learned was that voting was of great importance. When we turned 16, we were expected to drive people to the polls. Back then, most people were Democrats. So we brought Democrats to the polls to vote for Democrats. We participated in government and watched news conferences in my home.

What else did we learn? Obeying rules was paramount. We didn't get a chance to participate in the hippie movement of the 1960s. We had small sideburns. They were allowed to grow to the bottom of the ear. That was the limit or you weren't going to sit at the table that night. It wasn't going to be comfortable if your hair was not cut neatly and smartly.

Work and employment ranked high in our household. You always had a job no matter what else you were doing. If you were fired or quit or were laid off, you were not encouraged to take unemployment. You were encouraged to get another job right away. If it wasn't the right fit, something would come up along the way to make it the right fit, and you'd eventually have the right job. But sitting around waiting for the perfect job was not a Kelly family tradition.

We were a union household. We respected unions and we respected the efforts of people who worked. I don't think the system was abused the way ACORN and SEIU have abused it. We were both willing and proud to support union initiatives, such as better working conditions, higher wages and a better standard of living. All that has changed.

The unions now have a very different function. They serve in many ways as political entities, which was not their purpose when they first formed. The unions were noble. They were trying to keep people from having to work on Sundays, to get better wages if they had to work Saturdays. They set the work week at 40 hours, and Irish immigrant families needed it badly. This was especially true in Providence, because the city was home to hundreds of mills. There were mills of every type lining the streets, rivers and railroad tracks. They made everything from paper to jewelry, and anything having to do with metal, tools or machinery. Unions were respected in our home.

So that's what it was like. Those were the values taught to us by our parents and grandparents. It sometimes seems as if those values are gone, but they're not. They have worked out for me, and they live on in many other people I know.

If you have a "good" value system, does it keep you from making an error? No, you're going to make mistakes. But a good value system can help you recover. A big mistake does not have to be fatal, if you have a solid value system working for you and you know right from wrong. There's a price to pay if you want to step on the other side. So I think value systems work. They are survival mechanisms. They are ethics that allow us to navigate through life, and they're very important to have.

Back to Gramp. When I was 6 or 7, I remember going up into the attic and finding a toolbox. It was a black toolbox and it had every tool my grandfather had used back in the '20s and '30s. The box had a felt lining and the tools were all in bags. They were shiny and looked as new as the day they were made. Those were his tools from all his years of machining.

His suits all hung in the closet. He was a chicken farmer, but his suits were perfect. His shoes were shined and laid out in shoe trees. If we went to a family wedding or a First Communion, Gramp looked perfect. When he wore his blue suit with a white shirt and tie and his spit-shined black shoes, he looked like an older version of a *GQ* model.

It didn't matter what you did. What mattered was what you thought of yourself and how you conducted yourself. That was the value of looking sharp and the value of good grooming. For a man, keeping the fingernails manicured properly was very important. Gramp practiced what he preached.

I remember the day I got a call from my mother. It was 1979, and I was in New Mexico installing aviation computers. Gramp had to go into a nursing home and he was resisting. We'd had this talk over the years about the fact that I would never let him go into a nursing home. At the time my mom called, I was helpless to do anything about it. I had to fly to Boston in order to get back to help my grandfather. It took me almost a full day to get home. I got in at 3 a.m. and woke up at 9 a.m., wondering where Gramp was. I went up to his room and peeked in. He wasn't awake. Around 10:30, I went back up and this time he was. He looked at me then asked, "How are you, Murph?" (He had often called me that.) I responded, "Hi, how are you doing, Gramp?" He murmured, "Well, I guess we've got to make a trip today, don't we?" And I said, "I think we do, but, you know, how are you feeling about it?" In typical Gramp fashion, he said, "It's okay. Don't worry about it."

Gramp sat on the edge of his bed and got dressed the same way he always did. He wore the green pants he had bought at W.T. Grant, along with his two-pocket flannel shirt, white socks and black shoes. He came downstairs and drank his coffee while Mom called the ambulance. When the crew from the ambulance came up to the door, I turned to Gramp in pain and said, "I'm sorry." He looked directly at me and responded, "Don't worry about it. There's nothing we can do, so we'll make the best of this."

We got in the ambulance and I sat up with him. He actually sat in a chair that allowed him to sit upright. It was a big red ambulance and we talked on the way to the nursing home. As we rode down the country lane, I was changing. Every inch we traveled, my life was changing, my mind was changing and my spirit was starting to break. I didn't know what to do.

We got to the nursing home and Gramp comforted me with, "We're going to be fine. Everything's okay and this is a great place for me. Your mom and dad haven't had a vacation in three years." So we checked him in.

I saw him one more time, and then he was gone. I was in my 20's, trying to get a foothold in life and working halfway across the world. On my last visit, my grandfather was smiling and waving to me as I walked out of the nursing home.

Later, I heard that the nurses had dropped him and broken his ribs. He recovered from that, but they left him in his wheelchair in the shower on an icy winter day, then forgot about him. The hot water ran out, leaving him in an ice-water shower for hours. He developed pneumonia and died.

The last thing he had said to me was, "I love you."

CHAPTER FIVE

Kelly Feeling Bad

There is a lot of talk about teachers' pensions these days. Should we reduce them? Are they sustainable? What's going to happen? Who knows? My experience with teachers and schooling was a positive one. I think teachers are magnificent people. I don't want to get into how they're paid. I don't care what Tom Brady gets paid, but I enjoy watching him. I enjoy just *being* at the game. And that's the way I felt about my teachers. I had no clue what they were being paid, but they were very good to me. They taught me many lessons about life and they spent extra time with me. My folks didn't have to pay a nickel, other than their property taxes, in order for me to attend school.

I would like my children to attend parochial schools, some of which have a four-year waiting list. I want them to be able to attend these schools because the values taught are in sync with our family values. Yours might be different. Mine happen to fit the Christian values that are taught in the parochial schools. If my kids have to learn about things that are a little bit different nowadays, I can either take the time to teach them myself or else find out where else they can learn about them. I want to have as much control as I can. You may think I'm a control freak, but I'm not. We want to guard our children at a very young age and we want to make sure they have discipline and challenges. We don't want them exposed to things with which we might not agree. You can tolerate something or you can accept it. We tolerate and then we accept, hopefully. Tolerance transitions into acceptance if we find out the thing we've tolerated is actually benign, but there's a significant difference between the two concepts.

And where did I learn that? I learned that at the interview for my daughter's high school. There was a young man giving a speech about the difference between tolerance and acceptance. People will tolerate a lot that they do not actually accept. Being belligerent or mean-spirited does not promote either tolerance or acceptance. It may *force* people to tolerate something superficially in order to avoid fighting. Name-calling, finger-pointing, belittling or lying, however, will never result in acceptance. As I said, there's a big difference.

In my opinion, the value of life is the miracle of existence. If we belittle that miracle, then we devalue human life. There are people suffering, starving and dying on the African continent as we speak. AIDS is so widespread. Why don't we hear more about that? Why aren't we helping these people more? How do we do that?

Maybe we're going to have charities for overweight people now. Obesity is the new thing. Dr. Marc Lamont Hill appears on *The Sean Hannity Show* and pokes fun at New Jersey Governor Chris Christie for being fat. If you are on the Left, you have the green light to go after fat people and people in wheelchairs.

You're allowed to pick on people who are handicapped, and you get a pass for doing it. I don't think that really lifts us up as a nation, do you? I don't think that's part of spreading the wealth, do you? They can go ahead and make fun of fat people,

I guess. That's pretty much half the country. About 40 percent of Americans are overweight and I'm probably one of them.

We're attacking each other nowadays, my friend, and we're attacking with a goal. When people want to control you, the first thing they do is create factions to get you fighting. And guess what? When two people fight, one is going to vanquish the other. To control two people, all you have to do is to see to it that one beats the living daylights out of the other, and then control the one who wins. Now you've controlled two people. I think that's exactly what's happening in our current society. We are being controlled by pitting us against one another. I could be wrong, but I seriously doubt it.

Someone called my radio show and said, "This sounds like a therapy session, Kelly." I replied, "It is. It's a therapy session for me and maybe for some of you." For the most part, don't be ashamed of what's near and dear to you. If you have acquired something or if you've accomplished something, don't let anyone make you ashamed of your success. Exceptionalism is to be embraced because it leads to success, and success can be shared. You can help others while you help yourself. There is absolutely nothing to feel guilty about.

CHAPTER SIX
Mom Said It

Let's face it. Bill Kelly has gone beyond his time. He's shot. That's what I tell my family when I get home. "I'm shot, you know," and my 8-year-old son asks, "What's your point, Daddy?" I tell him it's time for him to go to bed and he asks again, "Daddy, what's your point?" It's obvious I am being treated too informally in my own house. That's what's going on. I'm going to put my foot down. Firstly, I'm going to severely limit their time on my radio show. Secondly, I'm going to severely limit the amount of chocolate stashed in the household. There is no doubt that we are over-chocolated.

That was one of Mom's worries: "You're getting all sugared up. You're sugaring up the kids!" If you went into her bedroom and looked underneath her pillow, you would find a package of those orange, marshmallow peanuts. Do you know the ones I mean? Or sometimes there would be peppermint patties. You could always find them somewhere in Mom's bedroom. It was unbelievable. I don't know how she kept a stash of candy safe with seven kids running around, but she did it. She had to choose her hiding place carefully, because she didn't want us kids "sugared up."

Television was called "the idiot box." That was one of Mom's favorite terms. She would ask, "Does the idiot box run this house?" And as a 9-year-old kid, I would think that it pretty much did run the house for me. It was my favorite place to be on Saturday morning, and I used to want to say to her, "Do we have to call it 'the idiot box,' Mom?" All I know is I looked forward to watching *The Cisco Kid, Hopalong Cassidy* and *Howdy Doody* every Saturday morning, and none of those characters was an idiot to me.

Coke was called "swill" and if you happened to be enjoying a bottle of Coke, Mom would ask, "What are you doing with that swill?" Obviously, she wasn't a big fan of soda. So "swill" was what you were drinking while you were sitting in front of "the idiot box." What other pet sayings did Mom have? "That woman is showing everything she owns." Mom meant that a woman was wearing too little clothing. "Showing everything you own" was something one of my teenage brothers wouldn't mind at all, but to Mom it was a terrible thing.

When she would argue with my aunts or sisters, it was coined, "I read them off." I have no clue what that means. If I happened to mention we hadn't heard from Aunt Eileen in a while, Mom would inform me that three weeks ago she had "read her off." That told us we were not going to see Aunt Eileen at Sunday dinner for a while. Eventually, they would make up and Aunt Eileen would reappear for Sunday dinner. Then we would naturally want to know what had happened when Mom "read her off." But we could never find out. To summarize, Coca-Cola was "swill," the television was "the idiot box," wearing revealing clothing was "showing everything you own," and if you had an argument with your sister, it was called "reading her off." So all these little issues are what we talked about at the dinner table.

Now, how did my mother judge a good man? There was one criterion and one criterion only. Both Elvis Presley and Wayne Newton met the criterion of being "good to his mother." Every time we saw either of those people on television—the "good" group, as she called them—she would say, "He sure was good to his mother." That often had the desired effect of making us all think about what we had done lately for Mom.

At Easter, we had to get her the most abundant blooms. On Easter Saturday my mind would race with, "We have to get extra blooms." We would bring home the lilies and the tulips and place them on the dining room table. The Easter blooms were then counted. There was some kind of magic telegraph that ran from Providence down to our house on the farm, so we knew the count of everybody's Easter flowers very early on Easter Sunday morning, before church.

I knew we were in trouble if we found out Aunt Charlotte had a lily with 14 blooms, and we had bought only five blooms from Woolworth's. If you had two separate four-bloomers and a tulip, you could offset a 14-bloom single plant, so we had to be on our toes at all times.

If we went to the potty, it was called "duty." Don't ask me why, but "duty" was never a topic of conversation at our house. Actually, there *were* no deep conversations. I didn't sidle up to Mom and begin with, "Well, you know, Mom, I've got some inner child issues." That wasn't done because there was another term Mom used fairly frequently. It was called a "backhander." If you're Irish and you have a family of more than three kids, you know what a backhander is. Today, a backhander would be considered assault on a juvenile and may have a jail sentence attached, but back then it was just something we watched out for. We measured the distance we sat from Mom, because we never wanted to sit under the gun, which was the first seat to the left of her. Why? Though she was right-handed, her left-handed backhander was stunningly accurate. But do you know what? We lived through it and it appears we all survived.

At the Kelly household, Mom delivered her colorful phraseology with a dialect heard on a daily basis. One thing I clearly remember her saying? "Don't lift your hands to me! Don't raise your hands to me when I'm hitting you! You're going to break my wrist." So raising our hands while getting whacked was the absolute worst offense we could commit. We could duck and imitate Muhammad Ali with head fakes and bobs, but generally Mom connected with one or two whacks. Once she delivered the two whacks, no matter where they landed, we were fine as long as we didn't raise an elbow or anything.

If we ever happened to be in Mom's bedroom trying to raid her candy stash, there would be her statue of the Blessed Virgin Mary, keeping watch. Underneath the statue was that lottery ticket for the Irish sweepstakes I told you about. We'd get those once a year. Dad played the numbers in a lottery pool. I believe it was the last four digits from Suffolk Downs, so you had to get the *Boston Herald* way down in Middletown, Rhode Island, every day to find out what the pool was. Dad would bet a quarter a day. Winners received about $600. Back then, that sum was enormous. Sometimes my parents would send me to a place in Newport with a little paper and some rolls of dollars to play the numbers, but generally it happened at work. There didn't seem to be a legal authority objecting to anyone's playing the numbers, except when the lotteries made their appearance. Then the number system had to go. So that was pretty much it for my parents' excitement. That and the dog races.

Once every two or three months, they'd take $12 or $15, go to Taunton or Raynham and have a great time. The hot dogs there were boiled with celery seed and mustard. That's how you ate a hot dog at the Raynham racetrack. There were working people by the tens of thousands. Can you imagine 15,000 to 18,000 people going to Raynham or Taunton on a Thursday night? You can't get 30 people to do something nowadays. But they'd come out to watch the dogs run, find stories to tell and release some frustrations. When my parents came home from the races, they would tell us for the next two weeks about the one that got away, or the dog that jumped up in the air or the dog that stopped to eat something. It was a colorful environment and the "Daily Double" was the biggest winner back then.

We had a housekeeper named Frances, who showed up on Saturdays. As I got into my teens, I would pick Frances up in my Ford Fairlane. I would leave the house about 9:30 a.m., pick up a dozen donuts and then get Frances. When Frances got to the house, she and my mother would have coffee and donuts. Can you believe that? Then, after a half-hour or so of refreshments, Frances would start working. Now Frances had one eye, and it was crossed. She had a glass eye and a crossed eye, so needless to say, the spray wax was always all over the place. My mother didn't care. Frances was part of the family.

She was in our weddings. Even our family group photos featured Frances, a cross-eyed black woman. She knew everything about everyone in town. At 12:30 p.m., Frances would have lunch, and my mother would always have special cold cuts for her. They would sit there and talk for about an hour, after which Frances would work some more. I have no clue what they paid Frances or how they paid her, but she got paid and everybody seemed to be happy. At 4 p.m., it was time to bring Frances home. We'd see her husband, Mr. Hennessy, and talk to him for a while before heading back. That was what Saturdays were like.

It was a time of colorful language and customs. We had safe homes, great meals and good lessons. Are we getting those lessons today? If not, is that something we can or should change?

The other day I was speaking with a couple who had home schooled their children. I believe they now have seven grandchildren, who are also being home schooled. They are going to introduce them into the school system as they approach high school, because they want to establish certain values and morals before the children are unleashed into the public-school sector. I think values are formed in the first eight years of a child's life. It's going to be difficult to make somebody a terrible person if they have been raised correctly. By the same token, it's going to be difficult to straighten out a child if good values haven't been properly instilled.

Values are like a radar scope, and they help us to detect when things aren't right. As children, we had values instilled in us, but the frenetic pace, the amount of activity and the different things happening at varied times in our house were maddening. It was amazing that we could all gather for dinner at 5:30 every night, but everyone was there for dinner. At 6:15,

Mom and Gramp would be sitting over a cup of Lipton tea and Dad would be reading the paper. Then the dishes were done, we children got our baths and were sent off to bed. It sounds like a dream or perhaps a comedy, but it did actually happen, 50 years ago.

❧

CHAPTER SEVEN
Mr. Pick

We used to have a man named Mr. Pick come by our house in his station wagon. I guess the best term to describe him would be the word "peddler." He arrived every two weeks on a Thursday, delivered the items my folks had ordered and took another order. This went on for at least 14 years, as I remember. Mr. Pick always carried the latest styles in clothing, though they would sometimes be a season or two behind.

When I was in grade school, the one thing I wanted most and begged for was a madras shirt. Do you remember when they were the rage? They were made out of a cotton fabric from India that would change colors when you washed it. So you never really knew what the bright plaid was going to finally look like until you had washed it a couple of times.

We would wash it by hand the first few times and then iron it with spray starch. I used to iron my own shirts in third and fourth grade, because we had a family of five kids and three adults back then. Richie and John had not yet joined us.

I remember asking Mr. Pick, "Do you have madras shirts?" He did, so Mom let me get my own madras shirt. I was really proud of that. Mr. Pick was a nice man. He had all of the latest clothing styles and made life easy.

We also had a bread man, believe it or not. I think his name was Hank. He would drive up to the farm in a big red bread truck and his company was called Arnold's Bakery. He was a handsome guy and looked like a movie star to me. The minute he arrived, we would climb into the truck, looking for his Toll House® cookies. They were something you couldn't get anywhere else. Needless to say, it was pretty exciting when Hank came. We'd all run up the lane. It was three-quarters of a mile to get to the farm, but whenever he'd turn off Paradise Avenue, which led up to the farm, we'd chase him. When he reached the house, he'd have either Toll House® cookies or hermits. The hermit was like a blond brownie. It had raisins and a certain cinnamon taste to it. We loved hermits.

There was a whole cast of characters who came to our farm. You remember Mr. Silveria, the chicken feed man, right? There was also the lumber truck that came with shavings for the hen coops. The Fuller Brush man, Mr. Blankenship, who would bring brooms, mops and cleaning supplies. We lived on a farm with now seven kids, my grandfather and my parents. Needless to say, the odors of the farm were generally not pleasant. So when Mr. Blankenship came and sprayed a few things around, it was like you were suddenly in Heaven. The Carters would come by for eggs and puppies from Minnie's most recent litter. Pete the barber would take any leftover puppies to his shop on Broadway and sell them for two dollars each.

That cast of characters is still there when I visit the farm in my mind, dear reader. The farm is long gone and it's hard to find the place where it once sat. My folks are in Heaven. They had great care until the end of their lives, thanks to Michael and Nancy, and never stepped foot in a nursing home. That doesn't mean I don't respect the people who work in nursing homes. They're dedicated, hardworking people whose jobs aren't always the most pleasant. It simply means my parents' wishes were important to my brother and sister.

Back then, there was no such thing as a trust for a poor Irish family. We couldn't even fathom something like that. It was all about work, work and more work. But people want to keep what they have, and I think that's the reason so many listen to my radio show. They want to keep what they have, use some of it and pass on what's left.

Mom would sell a piece of land every once in a while, to help her catch up on all the bills, and even get ahead on some things. She sent my brother to college on that money. It was as if my folks lived on their own bank. They could cut a slice of the property off, sell it and all would be right with the world. Back then, of course, the family car cost $1,200 and gas was 19 cents a gallon at the Gulf station. When I was in high school, my car was a 1957 DKW, which looked like a Volkswagen. Actually, it was the predecessor to the Volkswagen and required me to pour in gasoline and oil at the same time. Accelerating past 40 miles an hour was difficult, but could be done with some effort.

CHAPTER EIGHT
My Irish Mom

Apparently, the big rage out there right now is Chinese mothers, and how they raise superior children. So I'm wondering, what happened to the Irish mothers? And the Italian mothers, Jewish mothers and German mothers? I think they do a pretty good job, too. Jim Rice and Marco Rubio must have had great moms. As someone who has spent a lot of time in the Far East, I can tell you there are many sad people over there and one of their keen wishes in life is to come here and have what we have.

I believe the article about Chinese parenting was written by a woman for the *Wall Street Journal.* I don't know what's better about their parenting style and I don't want to get into an ethnic war here, but I *do* know about Irish moms. The author indicates the Chinese apparently are superior parents, in part, because they don't allow sleepovers. They never allow play dates. They do not allow their children to be in school plays. Their children are not allowed to complain. They do not let their children watch television or play computer games, and they do not allow their children to participate in extracurricular activities unless the parent has chosen them. Any grade less than an A is unacceptable. Their child must be the number one student or in the 99th percentile. This "tiger parenting" is common in East Asian cultures. So that's what makes them better than us.

In my family, I guess we were a little bit different. We slept over with our cousins constantly. Maybe that's how my folks got us out of the house so they could manufacture more kids. What happened if we didn't get all A's in school? Well, that was okay with my Irish mother, because we were taught that effort was important and respect for our teachers was important. We picked our own extracurricular activities. In school, what were mine? I worked on "Dollars for Scholars," which was a scholarship program for people who were less fortunate. I participated in many groups, such as the Junior Knights of Columbus, Student Council and Boy Scouts. I was class president, along with being a National Merit Scholar, and was a member of the National Honor Society and the Rhode Island Honor Society. My picture appeared in *Who's Who in American High School, 1971*. I ran track and played football.

No one really chose these for us. Our parents were too busy, and getting rides from my folks to any activity was out of the question. We bummed a ride or hitched a ride. Kids got wherever they needed to go on their own because both parents were working. It was part of the deal.

I was in the play *Brigadoon.* I was also in the choir and part of a madrigal group that used to go around to the nursing homes. Six of us in a choir group would sing and put on plays for those around us. I also loved caddying and learning poetry. So that's what we did back then. I mean, we were Irish and proud of our heritage and activities. I'm certainly proud of what I've accomplished.

So is an Irish mother better than a Chinese mother? I'm sure Chinese children love their mothers the same way we loved Mom. She was very loving in return, but she was also skeptical. If you have a lot of kids, skepticism is probably inevitable, because they are always coming at you with ideas. Her skepticism was helpful. It kept us balanced.

Whatever your mother's nationality, I hope you love her and she had a great impact on you. Our culture was great and we had a good time. My mom was half-Italian, half-Irish so we got the best of both worlds with her. Good food, good stories and sometimes a good spanking, too!

What did we learn? We learned that you had better try, you had better respect your teachers and you had better behave in church. We worked on the farm, we went to school and we loved our teachers. At home, we slept with a pile of puppies. Have I made mistakes? Sure, but I pray about those all the time, and I miss my mother.

CHAPTER NINE

The Value of a Paper Route

Everything I needed to learn about life I learned on my paper route. I can look back on just about any situation and discover I figured out what I needed to do from lessons learned on a paper route that began when I was 8.

The first thing it taught me was the importance of consistency. I had to show up every day, and that was something that was deeply ingrained in my character from very early on. Large families back in the '50s and '60s worked much like small factories. Everyone played a part, and if anyone didn't get his or her job done, then the other people would suffer.

I also learned how to interact with people and how to be dependable. I don't know how I ever did it in the dead of winter, especially towards the end of December, when it was dark by 4:15 p.m. There were some cold winters and I had to work through those winters.

The bicycle was my first vehicle. I remember thinking, as I was learning to ride my first two-wheeler, "Someday I'm going to have a paper route. Someday I'm going to make money using this bicycle."

"Someday" is a natural way to think when we're young. The boys in my family knew it was pretty much inevitable we'd have a paper route. My sister also had one for a month or two and then got scared, so we sold it to the Dobsons for $17 back then, and that was the end of it.

The Value of a Paper Route

The route entailed delivering 114 copies of the *Newport Daily News*. My first mode of transportation was not a van or an SUV. It was a Schwinn bike with balloon tires and three baskets. The two baskets on the back held the papers, and the basket on the handlebars held the paper bag, money collection sack and green record book. As I rode along, I would fold the papers a certain way, so I could actually approach a mailbox, open it, slip the paper in and flip the cover shut with my back hand without slowing down. My top time for finishing the paper route was 31 minutes and, believe me, that involved a lot of flipping of mailbox covers!

I had to pedal about 2½ miles to the drop-off point, which was the corner of Aquidneck and Prospect Avenues. We paperboys would all wait for the truck and the drivers who showed us no mercy. They enjoyed throwing the bundles of paper out the window to give us a hard time. The papers were wrapped in copper wire like a present, and if you were skilled enough you could grab it in a certain way and unwrap it by manipulating the wire. Then you would fill up your baskets with the papers. Eventually, the rules changed and we could no longer use the customer's mailbox. We had to use a special container that everyone was required to have.

When I was 9, I got a Huffy bike with dual baskets on the back for my paper route. To me, a Huffy bike was just about the coolest thing a kid could ever have. I used to polish it the way you'd polish the finest sports car on earth. To me, that bike was everything. I can remember as if it were yesterday, making sure the gears were oiled and the brakes worked.

Imagine riding down a snowy street on a three-speed Huffy bike in the middle of winter, with 114 newspapers to deliver. The headlamp was run by a generator powered by pedaling, so every time you stopped, the headlamp would go out. I had a reflector, of course, but it was very difficult to stop on ice with a Huffy. The bike would start to slide out from under me and I would have to try to land on the ground upright as my bicycle gave way beneath me. That was my largest problem in trying to get all those newspapers delivered in the middle of winter. My mom would help only if there was a torrential downpour of mammoth proportions. Otherwise, we were on our own. Just consider that for a moment.

The Huffy allowed me to deliver the papers and make more money, so I could perhaps buy another bike. With it, I could actually make a living. I learned to fix the Huffy when it broke down, and Gramp helped me to fix the flat tires. The common problems on that particular bike were the sprocket and flat tires. The sprocket was the part of the bike that transferred power from the chain to the back tire. On the original Schwinn bikes with balloon tires, it was pretty easy to change a sprocket. When you had a Huffy bike with a derailleur and three speeds, however, changing a sprocket meant bringing the bike to the bike shop.

The bike shop was at the bottom of our lane. Although I lived in a residential farm area, there was a shop that was essentially half a barn in someone's backyard. It was called "Everett's Lawnmower Shop" and I would bring my bike there, because Everett (I think his name was Everett Barker) knew how to fix any kind of bicycle, plus he could order sprockets.

While my bike was being repaired, he gave me a loaner. It was usually an old Schwinn with balloon tires. I would fill the tires and grease the chains. Next to Everett Barker's house was where Mrs. Barker lived. She was one of my customers for both the paper route and snow shoveling. As you can see, we had a little bit of a community there in which people helped each other.

The Huffy didn't hold up very well, so for my third bicycle I once again bought a Schwinn with balloon tires. The Schwinn was much better for doing the paper route. It didn't look quite as good as the Huffy, but it got the job done and also provided me with enormously strong legs by the time I got to junior high school. I was one of the quickest kids on the track team at that time. No one could figure out how I got such big calves until I told them about that Schwinn bike and what we had to go through year after year, delivering papers.

Times have changed. We have all but done away with the paperboys and papergirls of my day. First of all, their money would be stolen and their papers and bicycles would be taken from them. They could be kidnapped or otherwise harmed as they rode along. These days people deliver *The Boston Globe* and *The Providence Journal* in $40,000 cars, and make some money doing it, I guess. How do you give a tip to a person in a $40,000 car? We survived on our tips.

When I was 11, as I said earlier, I used to like to buy the three newspapers on Sunday, after church, and read them at home. I would pull out the "funnies" and the editorial page. I enjoyed reading about the president, his cabinet, our senator and all of that stuff. That's sort of going out the window today.

I would read *Blondie, Beetle Bailey* and *The Phantom.* Do you remember them?

Sunday was also the day for me to figure out my Red Sox batting averages for Pete Runnels, Carl Yastrzemski, Frank Malzone, Dick Stuart and others. We didn't have many pitchers of note back then, so I didn't spend a lot of time on ERA's; but I wanted to track the batting averages and follow the people coming up from the minor leagues. I was waiting for Joe LaHoud and others to be the next greatest sports phenomena.

I didn't have to deliver the Sunday paper, but I really enjoyed those three cartoons. Now they have pretty much gone the way of the dinosaur. As I said, times have changed. If we don't adjust to change as we move ahead, we're going to be subject to the whims of the marketplace.

For me, that paper route was a basic building block of my life. It allowed me to meet functioning, successful adults and their families. I looked into their homes every Friday night when I collected my money. I met the people and they paid me. And that's how I run my practice now, as far as fees go. People come in and if they like what I'm doing, they pay a fee. If they don't, they fire me. I think a pink slip at the paper meant someone didn't want the paper anymore.

So that's what it took, and that's what I did. Almost every life lesson in one form or another was learned on that paper route, and I can extrapolate from that even now. Wherever I was and wherever I traveled, it helped me to move forward through my life. I could always look back to draw on something from that paper route.

It was a formative, precious time for me. It was also a great time to be an American. Money handling, marketing services, sales, delivery, bill payment, record keeping and the maintenance of equipment – all learned on my paper route.

I don't know of any 8- or 9-year-old nowadays who could do that paper route and return home with the papers, the bicycle and the monies intact. One of the three would be stolen and the child, probably kidnapped. Back then, however, it was a great experience and I'm sure there are similar ones for young folks now. I learned a lot doing it. And, as it turns out, 114 people on a paper route were my first clients!

CHAPTER TEN

Paper Route People

Who were the people on my paper route? Well, the route began on Prospect Avenue, a tree-lined street where the arching branches actually formed a tunnel of sorts. The trees were thick, lush and old. My first client was a black family, the Hightowers. Mrs. Hightower was beautiful and they were all extremely kind to me. Both Hightower boys played football and were great athletes. Next, it was Mr. Kirby and his June Cleaver-type wife. Mr. Santos and his son were dairy farmers and they came after the Kirbys. The father lived in a small house out back and they tipped very well. They always took two papers.

I bought the route from Lionel Peabody, who told me it was the best paper route in New England. Lionel didn't exaggerate. Paradise Avenue ran along a brook. I could stop, grab a salamander, and bring it home to put in the aquarium or I could pick some raspberries as the summer wore on. The Peckhams' home had a lane leading up to the rock quarry. Mrs. Smith was the last house on Prospect and the first house on Paradise. Her house was right on the brook, and she was a wonderful customer, kind and very generous to me.

Heading down Paradise Avenue (as it was aptly named), I would reach Mr. Carlton Thorpe's home. He was a truly distinguished gentleman who, each Christmas, would present me with a Morgan silver dollar! There were other nice people on

Paradise, too. Mrs. Rooney had appeared on the Lipton Tea commercials. The Van Burens owned a large mansion, set about a half-mile back from the street.

Then I would change direction to deliver papers to some people who were both famous and wealthy. One customer was a lieutenant governor and another owned a lawnmower shop. You could stop at Barker's lawnmower shop and they would fix your bike or tighten up the brake. They'd spiff it up and never charge. I believe Mr. Barker had been Chief of Police in our town for many years. The Barkers' home was right on the brook and they had a bridge going over the water.

Mrs. Barker had a small roller coaster in her yard (I kid you not). It was about 50 feet long, and you could pull the silver car up to the top, climb up the ladder, sit in the car and push yourself off. You'd ride a mini roller coaster in her yard. Can you imagine that? The guys in the lawnmower shop used to keep the small roller coaster working. Nobody got sued. If kids got hurt on the roller coaster, they didn't go home and have their family call an attorney. It was a beautiful, rural setting in which the homes were gorgeous and well spaced. The last lane, Bailey Avenue, was where we lived. We originally had 27 acres, which devolved to about 7 acres over time. At that point, my folks finally sold it off, retired and left the farm.

As I said earlier, my collection night was Friday. I would generally get home around 7:30. Some people left money out in envelopes and some left it under the milk box. Some, like Mrs. Pedro, even waited for me. She'd hand me the money and say, "Okeydokes!" When I got home, Gramp was waiting. I had an orange bag with string ties that I would hand to him. I always went and washed right away because my hands were black from the newsprint. Then Gramp would count out all the money. He would sort the coins in separate bags, roll the money for the bank, and deposit it the next morning.

Saturday mornings I had to get up early to bring my money to the *Newport Daily News* office on Thames Street in Newport. During the week I worked every day after school, and still had to be there by about 8:30 Saturday morning. The paperboys lined up in the alley and there was a pecking order like there is with everything in life. We had to walk into the dirty, filthy money room. There was a man there with one leg, and he would take the money from us, open our bags, and throw the money into a big machine. It was the size of a big, old washing machine. You could see the wheels spinning and the coins would drop as it counted your money. A woman took the dollar bills and counted them. Together they determined whether or not you had the right amount. If you were short, you got a slip and had to bring the balance by the next week. And that's how it worked.

What did I learn? Well, obviously you have to count your money to make sure it's correct. You have to pay your bills, and you have to be accountable. I learned to have a healthy fear of authority, which I don't think is a totally terrible thing. To this day, I like policemen. I like authority. The lessons from a paper route are many. I don't see too many kids riding around on bicycles with newspapers anymore. Although I haven't bought a newspaper in three or four years, someone from *The Wall Street Journal* called the other day and asked me to do an interview.

That does not mean I'm going to pay $1.50 to read it. We have to get our ideas from our own research. We don't need the geniuses telling us what to do. If they knew what to do, they wouldn't be writing a column. They would own the newspaper.

All the things that went into having a paper route ended in time, of course. I sold my route for $37 to Peter Dobson. Who knows what he did with it? If I lived back on Paradise Avenue and my son or daughter asked me what to do for the summer, I would respond, "Why don't you get a paper route? Why don't you go house-to-house down our street and see what you can do with it? See what you can learn and see how wonderful life really is, getting to know the colorful people who live near Bailey Brook Farm."

CHAPTER ELEVEN

The Boy Scout Code

I was doing research on the history of Scouting in America and was amazed at how, from its inception, it has represented a fantastic gathering of American youth. I searched for and obtained a copy of the original *Boy Scout Handbook*. Written in 1911, it leads off with a message, in the form of an educational story, from Chief Scout Ernest Thompson Seton:

To the Boy Scouts of America:

There once was a boy who lived in a region of rough farms. He was wild with the love of the green outdoors – the trees, the tree-top singers, the wood-herbs and the live things that left their nightly tracks in the mud by his spring well. He wished so much to know them and learn about them, he would have given almost any price in his gift to know the name of this or that wonderful bird or brilliant flower; he used to tremble with excitement and intensity of interest when some new bird was seen, or when some strange song came from the trees to thrill him with its power or vex him with its mystery, and he had a sad sense of lost opportunity when it flew away, leaving him dark as ever. But he was alone and helpless, he had neither book nor friend to guide him, and he grew up with a kind of knowledge hunger in his heart that gnawed without ceasing. But this also it did: It inspired him with the hope that some day he might be the means of saving others from this sort of torment – he would aim to furnish to them what had been denied to himself....

This is very dramatic, isn't it? It's a book about a young boy who grows up in the woods, but he doesn't know about the stars, the birds, the fish or the insects around him. He makes it a quest for the rest of his life to learn about these things and pass the knowledge down. So this is the manual that he and others wrote to the youth of America. In this book there are, among other things, Scout virtues, the oath, the law, and the definition of a "tenderfoot." There are also lessons in woodcraft, canoeing, hiking, camping and chivalry, along with games and athletic standards, all in this book.

What does Scouting mean? Scouts have existed from the pass at Thermopylae to the various wars, and they exist in our current battle with terrorism. The scout was in the danger line of the army or at the outpost, there to protect others. They were scouts in peace and scouts in war, and "Be Prepared" was their motto. In 1911, they knew how to make beds from timber, weave cloth from rope and utilize other skills from the past.

One of the virtues of a Boy Scout is *courtesy*. Scouts should have a command of polite language and show they are true gentlemen by doing things for others. *Loyalty* is the second virtue mentioned. Furthermore, a Scout should refuse praise unless he knows he is worthy of that praise. Pretty amazing. Self-respect means that he cherishes those qualities God has given him, along with the gift of life. That's an interesting concept and something we don't think about much nowadays. In summary, the *Boy Scout Handbook* is a magnificent manual that incorporates practicality, principles and virtues.

The Scout of today must be chivalrous, manly and gentlemanly.
When he gets up in the morning he may tie a knot in his necktie

and leave the necktie outside his vest until he has done a good deed. Or he can wear his Scout badge reversed until he's done a good turn.

Knowing how to save a life was also important for Scouts to learn. They were taught to be in great physical condition and to have good hygiene. To be a good Scout was and is to be a well developed, well informed boy or young man.

The most important Scout virtue is *honor*. Where has that gone, dear reader? Honor is the basis for all Scout virtues. And it's closely allied to that of *self-respect*. When a Scout promises to do a thing "on his honor," he's bound to do it. *Faithfulness.* Where do we hear about that now? *Cheerfulness.* If you're going to do something, be happy about it. Don't go about things in a glum manner. *Thoughtfulness*, especially to those who are more helpless than you, is yet another.

There are many parts of this book that are interesting to me. When I was a Boy Scout, my handbook was a great guide. I can still remember the Code – the 12 points of the Scout law. *A Scout is trustworthy, loyal, helpful, friendly, courteous, kind, obedient, cheerful, thrifty, brave, clean and reverent.* Those seem like pretty good qualities to instill in children, even though the book was written more than 100 years ago. We need leaders who keep these tenets in mind. We elected one recently in Massachusetts, and we could use a few more to send down to Congress. If we do, we'll find that our country will start to improve. I want to go over the *Boy Scout Handbook* and the laws written when the Boy Scouts of America was created.

A Scout's honor is to be trusted. If he were to violate this by telling a lie, cheating or not doing a given task "on his honor," he risks being directed to hand over his Scout badge. *A Scout is loyal.* He's loyal to all to whom loyalty is due, including his troop leader, his home, his parents, God and his country.

A Scout is helpful. He must be prepared at any time to save a life, help an injured person, share duties around the house and do at least one good turn for someone every day. I think you will agree that's pretty good advice.

A Scout is friendly. Friendliness is the fourth virtue in the 1911 handbook. The Scout is a friend to all, and a brother to every other Scout. Pretty special, and yet the Boy Scouts are a group people are trying to have thrown out of public schools, because their bylaws offend the radical Left.

A Scout is courteous. He is polite to all, but especially to women, children, old folks and the weak and helpless. He must not take money for being helpful or courteous. I like that. *A Scout is kind*, the sixth virtue. He is a friend to animals and will not kill or hurt a living creature needlessly. He will strive to save and protect all harmless life. Michael Vick could have benefitted greatly from reading this handbook.

A Scout is obedient. He obeys his parents, Scoutmaster and all constituted authorities. *A Scout is cheerful.* He smiles whenever he can, and his obedience to others is prompt and sunny. He never shirks his duties, grumbles or complains about hardships. That was in 1911. We could use a bit more of that in this century. In fact, it sounds like the young military men and women who serve our country. They follow many of these principles, and I think that's why we admire them.

A Scout is thrifty. He will not purposefully destroy property. He works faithfully and does not waste. He makes the best use of opportunities. He saves his money and pays his own way. He is generous to those in need and supportive of worthy objectives. He may work for pay, but he may not receive tips or money for courtesies or good turns. Just think about that for a moment. Can we send this down to Congress and let them know this is the way we think our country should be run?

A Scout is brave. We know we have a lot of brave men and women in service to our country, beginning with local and state police, and working on up to our National Guard and our military. A Scout must have the courage to face danger in spite of fear and stand up against the coaxing of friends and the jeers or threat of enemies. Defeat does not hold him down. So a Scout is brave. What is bravery? Bravery is knowing that what you're doing might be dangerous, but doing it anyway. And it means being afraid, but doing it anyway.

A Scout is clean. He keeps clean in body and thought. He stands for clean speech, clean sport and clean habits, and he travels with a clean crowd. "Lookin' like a fool with your pants on the ground," as the man says and my daughter sings. Pretty simple. *A Scout is reverent.* He is faithful in his religious duties and respects the convictions of others in matters of customs and religion. The *Boy Scout Handbook* is more than 100 years old and it's something we've forgotten. We would be in much better shape if this Code were required of our legislators and they posted it and adhered to it. We need our legislators to be trustworthy and loyal to the Constitution and to us. Therein lies the big disconnect.

Americans don't like debt, really, especially not if they have worked hard to save their money. So being loyal and helpful to the constituency is important, if you're down in Washington working for the people who elected you.

Kindness. Have you seen an act of kindness from the leaders of the Senate and the House? I haven't. Obedience means adherence to the rules. *Cheerful.* I don't see a lot of cheerful people these days, do you? *Trustworthy.* Are the people in Washington who are cheating on their taxes trustworthy? Do you trust them? No. *Reverence?* Now *that* is almost laughable. I am reverent to the extent that I worship God and love Christ, but I'm not perfect, believe me. Far from it. I've had many troubles in my life. I've overcome them with God's help, and not because of any perfection in me. For that I'm very grateful.

We could run this entire nation by using the Boy Scout code of honor. And we'd be doing a pretty good job if we did only that. There are a lot of other tenets in the *Boy Scout Handbook* that would be wonderful for all of us to know. I think a code of honor ensures good character, from the time we are small children to the time we are getting ready to meet our Maker. A code of honor is a great thing to have.

Because I came across the *Boy Scout Handbook* just last week, I decided to present some of it, if only to help all of us remember the way things once were. It was okay to be square back then, and virtue was an admirable trait.

CHAPTER TWELVE
The Dream of Vaudeville

The other night I had a dream that was so realistic it was incredible. In the dream, I was walking in a flat meadow. It was a thick, thatched, vibrant green meadow with no hills, trees or flowers. In the distance, to my left, was a river. It was probably 20 yards wide. There was a corner at which the river changed course, and now it was flowing towards me with its gorgeous, deep-blue water. The air was still. The sky was blue. It was a sunny day, but not with a blinding sun.

I was walking through the meadow and looking along the riverbank to where the river changed course. Up ahead, there was a child sitting on the bank. As I approached him, I realized it was my son, William. I asked him how he was doing and he replied, "Hi Daddy, how are you?"

"There's somebody coming," he said, pointing downstream toward the other bend. There was a tall, gray-haired man there with broad shoulders, and I knew in a second who he was. I said to my son, "That's Tim Murphy, my grandfather. He's your great-grandfather. It's Grandpa Murphy." My son looked up at me and responded, "Really, Daddy?" I answered, "Yes, I think he's coming to talk with us." And Gramp approached.

Gramp had a slow gait most of his life. Actually, he took his time with everything he did. He was ambling along the river, taking his time. When he reached us, I hugged him and William ran up and took his hand. Gramp said, "Sit down, sit down. I want to talk to you. How have you been?" I could remember all the questions I've had every day of my life since he passed away almost 30 years ago.

There were things I wanted to ask him and I wanted him to recite some poems again, so William could hear them. I wanted William to know the stories of the Irish immigrants in Providence at the turn of the century and how they all operated when they got there. I wanted him to hear the jokes about the Irish people and the culture, and how Gramp used to call different people by different nicknames and tell us what they did. There was Mike Fox, who always wore a white shirt. No matter how foolish his endeavors, or how drunk or short of money he was, the "vite shurt" was the most important thing in his entire life to Mike Fox.

I wanted to hear about the fish peddler, the ice man and all of the characters he had told me about. I wanted him to relive every childhood experience he had. He used to tell us about Bishop McVinney and John Pastore, who were his choir mates at Blessed Sacrament Church.

Gramp said, "I don't have a lot of time, but I'm here to tell you some things and to give you some lessons to help you move ahead in your life." He sat us down and said, "Don't ever let God go out of your life." Then he looked at my son. "Don't you ever give up on your dreams. Finish what you start and keep your word to others and to God."

He looked over at me. "Save your money," and he reached in his flannel shirt pocket and picked out a passbook. "This is a passbook I wanted to give you, but never had the chance. I wanted to give it to you when we were in the ambulance going to the nursing home."

I replied, "You gave it to me. You did." But he handed it to me anyway. I remember looking at it. It was from the Industrial National Bank in Providence, Rhode Island.

We talked and he told me that even though life had dealt him some tough blows, especially during the Depression, he was not bitter. When the crash came, there were 12 people in his household, since his wife's parents lived with him in Cranston. The crash affected not only his business, but also the ability of his tenants' to pay rent. As you learned earlier, however, when the going got tough, Gramp got going.

As if to emphasize that fact in my dream, Gramp continued, "Don't ever give up. I want to tell you that this country, America, is the best in the world, and times are going to get tougher before they get better. It's a test, but they'll get better as we move ahead. We need to realize the best way to help people is to allow them to have jobs, families, housing, education, and the ability to live their lives freely and worship God. People *want* to work. When they have their jobs again, people will be a lot happier."

"So what you're saying is things are going to get better?" Gramp responded, "Yes. They might get a little worse first, but then they're going to get a lot better. Everybody needs to stick together." I remember thinking, "Wow, this is great. It's good to hear this." Then I asked, "What about me? How am I going to do?" He replied, "You've got to follow your path and you have to take care of your son. You have to stay true to yourself, to God and to your family. You're going to be just fine."

All at once, he began to sing an old Vaudeville tune and do a little "buck and wing." When I was a kid, he used to tap dance for me on the green linoleum floor in the kitchen. Picture a tall Irishman in his 70's, singing, tap dancing, and reciting verse to a small child seated at the table. Sometimes after lunch or dinner, he'd be washing the dishes and would decide to show me his act. Gramp used to work what were called the "smokers" in Vaudeville, so he could earn 25 or 50 cents. If you could do a three-minute act while someone else was changing, then you could earn some money and also have some fun.

So in that verdant meadow, Gramp began to tap dance and sing an old Vaudeville song, and my son and I just sat there, watching him in awe. Then he slowly faded into the background, dancing and singing. I remember thinking then, "Boy, I wish we had more time to talk." But the message from the dream was clear: *Things are going to get better. It's going to be a little tougher than we might like in the meantime, but they are going to get better.*

It was an amazing dream and it seemed real. When I woke up, I remember finding a box with an envelope full of pictures and family mementos my brother Walter had shared with me over Christmas. I opened the big manila envelope and looked through it for the first time in about a year. Since I had been meaning to sort it, I dumped the contents on the desk. There were some school pictures, and one of Gramp at a wedding.

There were pictures of me in second grade, in addition to some other mementos, and there was a canceled passbook containing pages filled with transactions. It had been stamped with a machine that made holes in it and the cover read,

"Industrial National Bank." I opened it up. On the inside cover was Gramps' name, Tim Murphy. I stared at it for a moment. It was the passbook from my dream.

That discovery validated the message about our being "okay" in life. Gramp said we're going to get back on our feet, dear reader. It's going to be a little challenging to do that, but we're going to get back on our feet. God, family, home, school, work and play, components of the American Dream, are going to be restored. I believe it's a great dream for all of us and we can make it happen for everyone by working together, which, in the end, we will do.

CHAPTER THIRTEEN

What It Means to be Irish

What are the most important values I have learned as a result of being Irish? Perseverance and the ability to fight back. The social, economic and political issues we are dealing with today are the same types of issues that confronted my ancestors in Ireland. Cromwell basically wanted to eradicate the Irish. Because of that, he created a really traumatic environment for my ancestors, who were raped and slaughtered by his men.

An interesting part of Irish history goes back to Sts. Patrick and Brigit. St. Brigit created a series of monasteries in Kildare, Ireland. She was given her orders from St. Mel, who I believe was the nephew of St. Patrick. She set up monasteries for both men and women, who flocked to them during one of Europe's darkest periods, when the culture was under assault. Its history and literature, its very underpinnings, were being burned. Muslims were attacking from every direction (sound familiar?), so people would go to the monasteries in Ireland to study, pray and write. They would translate and transcribe in the monasteries founded and built by St. Brigit of Kildare, preserving writings that would later become the foundation not only of Irish culture but also of a significant part of Western civilization. Many miraculous things happened in those monasteries.

The census was a terrible weapon in Ireland. Its main use was to find out how many people were in a home, so the government could steal their resources and then deal with them after they had robbed them of their property and their dignity. If there were fewer Irish to contend with, the British would be able to take more of the land and dedicate it to the queen. England was a colonizing nation, constantly on the lookout for more territory to control. In the crosshairs were India, North America, Canada and the Virgin Islands.

To colonize these areas and send out forces, the British had to have supplies, so they plundered Ireland for lamb meat, wool and potatoes. Ireland became a place where the British could rape the land and rape the people. They took more and more until eventually, in the 1830's and 1840's, it began to backfire. It backfired because Ireland sank to such a level of impoverishment that it couldn't sustain the demands of the Crown or even support its own people. There wasn't enough food. One million people starved and millions more left their country. Ireland was broken by the filthy Cromwell.

Most Irish families had a one-room home with a hearth, and sometimes they would keep a farm animal in the house with them so nobody could steal it. They would sleep in cradles and bunks. That's what they went through. You may see a lot of wonderful movies such as *Darby O'Gill and the Little People* and *The Quiet Man,* they are fairy tales at best. It was a tough time for the Irish, and nobody cut them a break.

There was a sport in Ireland for the British constables and sheriffs. That sport was eviction and it was a spectator sport. The only piece of equipment needed was a pole about 30 feet long, with a pick at the end. The idea was to climb onto people's roofs and stick the pole through the thatching, in an effort to stab whoever was in the way.

When people saw the spears coming through the roof, they would run out of the house. As soon as they had escaped, the British would bar the doors. Then the sheriffs would go in, throw out all the furniture and board up the doors. Anyone who tried to return would be arrested. So some people lived in the brush and some lived in caves. I have pictures of some of my cousins standing in front of a cave in the late 1850s. That's where they lived when the British came around. Their hope of coming to America was a distant dream.

The people who did make it to our country thought they were in Paradise, because there was food and plenty of work, though it was tough work. I have a picture of my grandmother Kelly (her maiden name was Moore), from the Donnybrook district in Dublin. My Kelly ancestors came from Roscommon, Ireland. They went to Liverpool, England to work in the mills because their fare was paid. Once they saved up some money, they came to America. From 1851 to 1879, various Kellys came from Roscommon to America via Lancashire and Liverpool. Some of the Kellys ended up in the Springfield and Ludlow areas. The Murphys wound up in Providence. We had arrived in this wonderful place called the United States of America.

CHAPTER FOURTEEN

A Moral Compass

Competition is viewed through a very negative lens these days. We want to eliminate competition because it hurts people's self-esteem, even though the difference between the top golfer in the world and the person who is number 300 on the tour is approximately four strokes for 18 holes. Four strokes. Can you believe that? How people fare in match play and react to tournament pressure determines who wins. It's a razor-thin margin. To continue the nonsensical logic, it's also the people who save $10 a week during their lifetime and add to it when they get raises and bonuses who are now the target for massive tax increases. People who save, who invest wisely, who watch their money and who have accumulated it are going to be hit hard. But there are some ways to combat this, and potential ways to save your estate from parasitic taxes. We're well versed in those ways.

So that which we feared is here. We are losing our liberty and having policies forced down our throats, crafted in part by people who have lived on the public dole as "public servants" all their lives. These are people who have stolen our money in front of our very own eyes. Our government has decided the best way to have healthcare for all is to control every aspect of it.

The IRS is going to have access to your medical records, dear reader. They're going to know how much and where you pay for medical insurance, and they alone will decide whether it qualifies or not. If it doesn't, they will assess a penalty. Then they will determine when and how they're going to collect it. What does that mean? For starters, that means neutralization of your tax rebates. That means liens on your home. It means getting in your face, in a manner of speaking.

Now I, personally, am not a tax protestor. I withhold taxes at an outstanding rate because it's my fair share. This is America and I am free. Well, kind of free these days. But it's reaching the limit for me. It's becoming increasingly more difficult to pay $3,000, $4,000, $5,000 or $6,000 a week in taxes. That's a *lot* of money. The first year I started in the finance business, I made about $4,900. Then I made $12,000. Then $34,000, $65,000 and I think I made my first $100,000 back in the '90s. I've been fortunate every year to have made more money. Don't ask me why, because halfway through a lot of those years I thought, "Geez, I'm not going to make it this year. This will be the year."

Along the way I've had to pay increasingly more taxes, and guess what? I'm glad to do it. We have our share of audits at my business, all successful. The IRS treats me very well. I just don't think they are who I want monitoring my health insurance and healthcare. I think they ought to stick to taxes, and I think we ought to be able to choose our own medical care, because we definitely need to be insured. Actually, the things we really need were never in the government's plan. Come to find out, they "forgot" things that were in the legislation. If I remember correctly, we were told they had to pass the bill in order to find out what was in it.

It's like those grab bags we could buy for 25 cents at the penny candy store. Do you remember them? The mystery bags were fun and you wouldn't find out what was in them until after you bought them. Sometimes you were happy and sometimes you felt like you got gypped. Well, we have a mystery bag that's been opened for us. We paid about $10 trillion for it, and I don't think we're exactly euphoric with what's in there. Remember how our taxes were going to quickly decrease and healthcare costs were going to plummet? Those turned out to be terrible lies.

If you are diabetic or someone who needs a wheelchair, then you're going to be taxed every month on what you need. And if you pay more than seven percent of your income for your supplies or medicines, something that used to be deductible, guess what? The qualifying deduction has been increased to 10%. So lower-income people are hurt. It doesn't hurt people who are making $200,000, $300,000 or $400,000 a year. It hurts the average person.

You agree that something has to be done? That you have to create a defense against this? How do you defend your estate? You put a moat around it with a drawbridge, and then you put barbed wire around the turrets. You might want to get a pot of boiling oil in order to prevent the government from coming to take what is yours. The instinct to protect your estate harks back to early Europe. The estate was the place or the manor where the monied people lived. It takes a long time to create an estate. You don't want it wiped out by a tax mistake that will hurt you or spoil a great retirement.

One of my son's favorite books is *Mike Mulligan and His Steam Shovel*. His steam shovel is named Mary Anne. Back in the early '20s and '30s, believe it or not, many of the machines were female. *The Little Engine That Could* was actually a female. Mike Mulligan and Mary Anne would travel from town to town, even after steam shovels were obsolete. They would travel the countryside and find work. Now the thing about Mike Mulligan and Mary Anne the Steam Shovel was that they would work a little harder and a little better if people were watching. Whenever people would gather around when they were digging a basement or a town hall, they worked harder and better. And they loved having people watch them. Basically, they're the opposite of our Congress. *They* don't care who is watching. *They're* not going to work harder, and *they're* not going to work better. They are going to give up and give in to political chicanery and insider dealing. Mike Mulligan's instinct is similar to that of the American people. When we're up against it and we need to pull ourselves up by the boot straps, we work a little harder and a little better. And this is especially true when the world is watching us or people are depending upon us.

Now it seems there are a group of people who think we can't make it. They're absolutely wrong. Those are the mocking fools, remember? The mocking fools tell us we're racist. They say white people in trucks are terrorists and policemen are racial profilers. And how do the people in Washington right now deal with us? If they think you're a square, if you drive a truck, if you work in construction, if you're a veteran or if you're retired from a career in law enforcement, you are viewed as a potential domestic terrorist. Very twisted thinking.

What threat do you pose? The threat you pose is that you have a brain, dear reader, and you know right from wrong. That is a bad thing and a dangerous thing to these people. If you know right from wrong, then you definitely know that killing a baby in the eighth month of its development probably isn't something to brag about and promote. In their eyes, then, you are a person who has something wrong with you. They want to do something to silence you, to eradicate you, to take away your sense of modesty and your sense of decency. So they mock you. They deliver verbal assaults. And the mocking fools don't pull any ratings. Nobody listens to them. Nobody's interested in them, but they are there to let people know there is someone to turn to. The mocking man is going to stab us in the back. He has no intention of voting against a bill that gives a legal wink and a nod to late-term abortions funded by you and me. He's fooling us. He's deceitful. He can turn on Chris Matthews and be comforted by hearing there are terrible people who believe a child's life begins when he or she is formed in the womb.

We can also find people on television who tell us they are going to sue Tim Tebow's mother. A commercial was made for the Super Bowl in which he says, "Thank you, Mom, I love you." And his mom said, "Boy, he was a *handful* when he was a kid." So Gloria Allred decides to sue Tim's mother for fraud. The only fraud is Gloria Allred herself. She's an ambulance-chasing weasel and she's out there telling us what a terrible person Tim Tebow's mother is, that she made a false claim so she should be sued. There were actually people trying to stop that ad from running during the Super Bowl! As a nation, we have lost our moral compass to the Gloria Allreds of the world and their bottom-feeding ilk.

Tiger Woods gave a press conference in which he looked like an angry man venting at the people around him. He did the most hideous things. His behavior was despicable! Is it any of my business? Actually, it's not. He's a golfer, and I don't care. Believe me, I seriously don't care. So I guess the golfers of the world are going to have to forgive him. Tiger's ex-wife couldn't, after finding out he was texting and consorting with all these other women. Maybe he's learned his lesson and things will be different with Lindsey Vonn.

So this is what the Left are doing. They're trying to dumb you down. They're trying to get you not to wince every time you hear about a late-term abortion, a woman killing her baby. When we hear about that, we're supposed to be anesthetized. And if we see people who love their parents on a commercial for the Super Bowl, then why do we need folks on *The O'Reilly Factor* telling us it's tantamount to slavery? All Tim Tebow did was simply to tell his mother what a great mom she was: "Thank you for having me despite the risks. I love you, Mom." He's a millionaire, and he deserves it. He's a great kid who works like the dickens and deserves every dime he makes.

So you need to keep your compass with you at all times. North is still north and south is south. Keep that in mind, friend. There's nothing wrong with being a square. There's nothing wrong with the *Boy Scout Handbook*. Every major politician and leader in America, from Teddy Roosevelt to the CEOs of large companies, with one notable exception, both signed on to it and endorsed it. And there's a reason for that. It's full of American civic values. It shows people how to be not only great Americans, but also great human beings.

Wait a minute. I shouldn't say "good" or "great" Americans anymore because that's a slur. "Exceptionalism" is a dirty word these days. But we know what good Americans are and we know what they do and how to recognize them. The first thing they do is put their hands over their hearts and say the "Pledge of Allegiance" straight up, including the phrase, "One nation under God," and they have no qualms at all about doing it.

CHAPTER FIFTEEN

My Prayer in the Woods

O ur son, William, blessed us by arriving somewhat late in life. My wife, Kelly, was very courageous. We decided from the "get-go" that he was going to be our joyful package. I can tell you right now that I haven't had a bad day since his birth. We've been blessed.

According to the U.S. Census Bureau, between 77 percent and 83 percent of our country are Christians. And it's a fact not all Christians or churches are consistently pro-life. But overall, we are a pro-life country, no matter what you hear to the contrary. From a personal perspective, I can tell you my clients were very excited about this child. We brought William Kelly Jr. to Ireland eight weeks after he was born. My son was baptized in Dublin at Saint Teresa's Church, the very same church in which my grandmother was baptized in 1879.

He has grown up with a good attitude. He's a gamer and he listens to his dad, for sure. I'm proud of our relationship. I wasn't always the way I am today. I wasn't always this grateful nor was I always as attentive to how well things have gone in my life and the reasons for that. William Kelly Jr. is a gift to me, to our family and to the world. He's just a great kid.

We were at the playground one Thursday a few years back. He loved going to the playground, because there he would meet other children that he called "my friends." It was a great thing for him and is actually a great feeling for everyone when we have a person, or people, around us whom we view as true friends. Though they are few and far between, you know them if you have them. You might have one or two. If you have any more than two, then you are already in Heaven, because you're living a dream.

When the children had all left the playground, William was a little wistful. He walked over and sat on the bench, then said, "Don't worry. There's nobody here now, but my friends will be here again soon and we're going to have a lot of fun." Just ponder for a moment the process that creates those thoughts in a child's mind.

They reflect optimism, love, and faith in other people. There is no sadness or loneliness after everyone has left. William was just looking ahead to when the next group of people, whom he called his friends, was going to be there. The joy of life is continuous and replenishes itself for him. Very small disappointments are sprinkled in around the joy, here and there, because it's life, after all. But you'll agree that was very profound thinking for a boy of 5.

My early business years were a struggle, but I had a mentor. He was a Jewish man, an attorney in Springfield. He's almost 93 now and his name is Leonard Michelman. He would call me from time to time, subtly checking on how I was doing by asking me what was going on in my life and how things were going in general. Then he would give me some advice. Leonard was a lawyer who never took anyone to court, because he had a natural way of settling things.

He'd scare the dickens out of whoever was bothering me and he'd scare the dickens out of me, too. He'd say, "Let's get it settled. Why are you arguing in the first place? The purpose of money is to create happiness, and if it's creating sadness then there are a lot of things you have to look at, concerning what's happening in your life."

When things started to go well, he called me one day and I asked him, "Is there a prayer, Leonard? Is there a Jewish prayer for a time in your life when things are going very well after a time of trial?" Leonard replied, "Oh, sure there is. I have it here. It's under the glass on my desk." I asked if there were any way for me to get a copy and he told me he'd fax it over to me. So he faxed me a prayer, but it was written in Hebrew. I called him and thanked him for the prayer, but told him I couldn't read it. He said, "I didn't know you wanted to read it. You just asked me if there was a prayer." I asked him if he would write out the words phonetically for me, so I could say the prayer. He did exactly that and faxed the result to me. In my filing cabinet is a manila folder labeled, "Jewish prayer."

I took the prayer and went down to a small stream in the woods, got on my knees and said the prayer out loud on a sunny summer day. The sun shone through the rich green treetops and reflected off the pool formed by the brook. And I thanked God. The prayer went something like, "Thank you, God, for the adversity you gave me. And thank you again that the adversity is behind me now and I'm so much stronger. But if I hadn't had the adversity and the hard times, I would never have realized how great things are and how strong I am now. And so I thank you, God, for the adversity, and I thank you for the blessings that have come after that adversity."

So, my friend, that was the lesson. And what do I do now on behalf of my son? I try to fight the universe so he won't suffer adversity, even though that might not be the best thing for him. Maybe teaching a young man to overcome adversity is a better idea. Gramp used to say, "I never want you to walk around with your hand on your ass. It's a terrible feeling to depend on others and not know if you're going to be okay."

I think about that when I think about my son, my wife and my daughter. How can we help our children persevere through adversity and come out the other side? I want William to get to the other side, so someday he can recite the prayer and say, "Thank you for the adversity and thank you for the tough times, Lord. Thank you for giving me the ability to make it through and the sense to realize how strong it has made me. Thank you for the challenges and thank you for the rewards, Lord!"

CHAPTER SIXTEEN

The Proper Use of Power

Hope is important. I was doing some online research on motivation recently, and rediscovered a gentleman who wrote some principles of success about 120 years ago. He said one of the key things in life is understanding *the proper use of power is to help others.* How do you like that? Most of our clients embody that thinking. If you have investments or an estate, you want to pass it along to those you love. So the proper use of power is to help others and probably that's the proper use of your estate as well.

Another principle this gentleman lived by asks us to *give up something we want in order to help someone else.* Sacrificing now in order to make your life better in the long run can be a good thing. Believe me, in my years of practice I've seen people who have delayed gratification for 55 or 60 years. Why? They want their children to have a better life. They want to help them get through medical school or to send them to private schools or Catholic schools. They give up many things and they sacrifice.

A third principle of success is to learn how to *challenge and overcome doubt and fear.* We all have experienced those feelings at one time or another. If you've raised a family, you know what it's like to get out of bed in the middle of the night and go out to get medicine for a sick child. It's raining or gloomy, and you drive down a dark street, looking for the all-night pharmacy. You purchase the prescription or the cough medicine, whatever is necessary to make your loved one feel better. We do what is right to help others.

Learning how to use knowledge wisely is yet another solid principle to live by. It's true that a little knowledge can be a dangerous thing, but knowledge tempered with discipline and a generous spirit manifests itself in helping others. By so doing, we maintain gratitude. *Making gratitude a part of every thought and action* is another principle of success. Both gratitude and knowledge are intertwined in estate planning and investment planning. "I want to keep what I have, and I want to pass on what's left. I want to use what I want. I want to grow my investments a little bit." Those are the goals of a proper plan and that is what many people are doing. If you want a will and trust workbook or an estate tax guide, you can call me at 1-888-800-1881 and I will send it to you at no charge.

A further principle of success is *practicing the skill of listening before making a judgment.* Remain true to your word. If all our politicians did the latter, how good would you feel? Practicing the art of *giving without expecting something in return* is very difficult for me. What if we could all be generous of spirit? Just think about that for a moment.

Your personal success is as much a motivation to others as it is to you, and vice-versa. Everyone is motivated by success when they know that they can make a difference in someone else's life.

So who wrote these principles of success? A man named Frederick Douglass. He was a United States ambassador, and was very influential during the Lincoln administration. By the way, Douglass was an African American. He grew up a slave, but became one of the greatest orators of all times and was a truly inspirational man. Indeed, I love reading works by Douglass. It was against the law for him to learn to read, but he did it anyway. Douglass saved his lunch scraps and traded them in to the plantation owner's kids in exchange for some books to read. Frederick Douglass became one of the most well-respected speakers during the second half of the 19th century. If you'd like to have a copy of his *Principles of Success,* call our toll-free number and we will send you one, again at no charge.

So Frederick Douglass was born into slavery in 1818, forbidden to learn to read or write, and later became one of the most famous American orators and statesmen. I'm proud to say he was an American, and I'm proud to say I believe his principles are germane even now. I am energized by the fact that a person like Frederick Douglass, who lived long before me, can still inspire me.

Frederick Douglass' Principles of Success

I. The Proper Use Of Power Is To Promote The Common Good.

II. Give Up Something You Want In Order To Help Someone Else.

III. Overcome Doubt And Fear.

IV. Understand Why And How To Control The Human Ego.

V. Do What Is Right And Proper Even If No One Is Looking.

VI. Use Knowledge And Understanding Wisely.

VII. Overcome Indecisiveness.

VIII. Make Gratitude A Part Of Every Thought And Action.

IX. Practice The Skill Of Listening Carefully Before Making Judgments.

X. Remain True To Your Word.

XI. Hold A Vision For The Desired Future.

XII. Recognize That Your Success Is As Much A Motivation To Others As To You.

CHAPTER SEVENTEEN

Tim Murphy, Part One

I have the expired Industrial National Bank passbook from the early 1970s in my left-hand drawer. I was sitting with Gramp one day, when he was very ill. Reaching into his pocket, he handed me that passbook, saying, "Give this to your mother." I put it in my top shirt pocket without saying anything, and as I was leaving, I gave it to my mom. "Gramp wanted you to have this." He had saved money at that bank for many years and his passbook was marked with small, typed black lines.

Every time he had saved $1,000, he would apparently move it to another account somewhere else for a slightly higher interest rate. Gramp had turned that passbook into his own personal money market account. It's kind of interesting to flip through and see how he used it, knowing him as I did.

Gramp was essentially a gentleman chicken farmer. He had perfectly pressed suits, neat ties and immaculately shined dress shoes. His beautifully tailored overcoat was made of camel hair and was always stored in the closet with mothballs, to keep it from being eaten. Two days before an upcoming event, be it a wedding, a First Communion or a funeral, Gramp would take the coat out of the closet and hang it on the outside of the closet door, or maybe in the yard someplace, for an hour or two to get rid of the camphor smell associated with moth balls. Then he'd groom it to a fault with a boar's hair brush and off he would go to the event. That was Gramp. Even though his post-Depression journey saw him morph from a manufacturing scion to an egg farmer, he never abandoned the gentleman within.

If you're ever in Providence and you walk out the back door of the Providence Performing Arts Center, there's a city block there that Gramp owned. I think he had 16 apartment buildings on that block when times were good.

Insurance companies financed buildings that Gramp and his buddy, McDermott, would construct. They had a set of pictures made up and sent them to whoever was financing them, in order to get progress payments for each project. Gramp and McDermott didn't take different sets of progress pictures. They used the same set. Sometimes they flipped them over and the developer would shoot the negative backwards so it looked like different buildings. They ended up with a lot of apartment houses. Gramp also owned a large interest in a firm that made change-counting machines and then that, too, was gone.

Demand for his enameling services disappeared because DuPont introduced new, epoxy-type substances to replace the enameling that was relatively expensive to do back then. The old badges and the REO Motor Car Company emblems were all made by my grandfather. So he had built up quite a family, had 36 apartments and had become wealthy. After the crash, however, he found himself in a business with no demand, sitting on the East Coast of a nation that was broken.

During the Depression, Providence looked like a prison camp. People would sit on their stoops all day with nothing to do. Gramp had eight children and no one to pay the rent in his apartment houses, but, as I said earlier, he didn't collapse in a pool of self-pity. Instead, he started working every kind of job he could. This once-multimillionaire delved into painting bridges and schools. He did carpentry and worked in machine shops such as American Standard and Brown & Sharpe. Gramp was now a blue-collar worker, and a darned good one at that.

I told you about my finding Gramp's box of tools in the attic and how they looked brand new because he took such good care of them. He did machining into the '40s and then had a terrible accident. Some machines fell on him, along with a pile of chains from the ceiling of the shop. Dr. Bestoso wanted to remove his leg. Gramp refused and recovered miraculously, but couldn't stand on his feet for extended periods anymore.

So he and my parents bought the farm and Gramp decided to build hen coops and raise chickens. My folks worked. Gramp did the cooking and laundry and took care of the chickens. We never needed a babysitter, because we had Gramp. Life was good.

Gramp was my advocate. He and I became very close. I see a lot of Gramp in William. He eats meals very slowly, the same way my grandfather did. He never opens his mouth when he's eating. He focuses and he likes to talk.

When William was 5, he and I went to the baseball batting cages. He was starting to hit off a tee. We finished and while I was paying the owner, William was over by the break area, at the age of 5, talking to the high school baseball players, who were all talking to him. There's a twisting movement that a beginning batter does with his back foot. It's called, "stepping on the bug." You have to twist your back foot and pivot your hips and that's how you develop your stride eventually. The movement teaches a beginner to open up the hips at the right time. So

William is talking to these teenagers about "stepping on the bug" and I notice a camaraderie and respect between him and them. He is learning to be a young man with other young men.

One of the things I like about going to the batting cages is meeting the type of kids who play baseball. It's an amazing sport and seems to attract good kids. The team practices, the uniforms and the traditions are just so American, you know? Some people on the Left get offended when I use the term, "so American," and they get ticked off because I love America and traditions like baseball. They probably need to switch the radio station when I am on the air. I'm sure there are other programs that are more in keeping with their twisted ideology.

Back to youth baseball. If William continues playing, he will meet some great kids. As for his demeanor, again, it is a lot like that of my grandfather, Tim Murphy. William is deliberate, smart, steady and focused. He is constantly moving ahead and making progress. I love it, and I love the spirit of those young baseball players. I am glad my son gets along with them and that he will be playing baseball someday. I know he'll be better than I was, because he started early.

In the spring, when I got my baseball glove ready, there just weren't that many people around to play with me. Sometimes I would hit the ball to myself. Sometimes I would throw the ball against the side of a shed. I'd get old tennis balls and hit myself grounders, but I never really could play the game well. I loved it, though. I used to keep score and listen to the Red Sox games when the team went on their road trips to the West Coast.

I remember listening to Curt Gowdy on the radio late at night, under the bedspread with my dog, Minnie. I would fall asleep with my transistor radio beneath my pillow, pencil in hand. The very next morning at breakfast, I would have my cereal and talk to Gramp about the game. It was a great life.

CHAPTER EIGHTEEN
Tim Murphy, Part Two

We decide that we love life. People love us and we love them. We want to be with people we love. It's another piece of evidence that we don't exist as islands of humanity.

The first breath we take in life is probably involuntary. If we're lucky enough to be born healthy and move ahead in time on Earth, every breath we take after we reach the age of consent is basically voluntary. Between the first breath and the last one, a lot of things happen. Some of those things might seem like a miracle and some, like a curse. But we are a collection of people who love life, obviously, or many of us would just quit and give up. We could take a survey and ask people if they are in favor of living. If we compare the number of people who decide to participate with the number of people who decide to opt out on any given day, we would have to admit the survey overwhelmingly points to the fact we prefer to live, with all the pain and all the joy that living encompasses.

We can have doubts, we can have hopes and we can have dreams. I grew up on a farm. The strongest human being I ever knew was Gramp. He would sit me up on the table and tie my shoes, then out I'd go to my domain, the farm. I had my own trees, my own stone walls and my own brook. I could play. Many children today, including William, need a lot of face time. He needs me there, and I don't mean just sitting in the same room working on my computer while he works his iPad. That's not going to cut it. That's not face time. He needs me to participate in an activity with him. If I do that for 20-40 minutes, we can sit in the same room without the need to be facing each other. If I don't do that, then he's constantly in need. Since he's the best friend I've ever had, I don't mind doing it at all. He's a great human being who happens to be my son and I love him.

When I was about 3, I had a little routine during the early morning hours on the farm. It was a bad thing to do and I admit it, because it was deliberate and preplanned. I couldn't help it. You've heard of compulsive gamblers? Well, I was a compulsive cookie eater.

How did it work? I slept in the same bedroom as Gramp, in a crib with a top my father had made. It had a screen and it had latches all along the edge, to keep me from getting out. Over a period of time, however, I was able to create a bit of a hole in the crib screen that no one could see but me. I would poke my hand through and undo the latches.

Somewhere around 5 a.m. each morning, I would escape, all the time making sure that Gramp was still asleep. After landing on the chair where he had left his green work pants and flannel shirt, I'd step onto the floor, walk into the kitchen, and go to the kitchen table. Then I'd slide a chair over to the cabinet that had the cookies in it. Since it was padlocked, I had to climb onto the counter and reach on top of the refrigerator, so I could get the key to open it

I remember stretching up to the top shelf, where there were bags of cookies. I took the number of cookies I wanted, closed the cabinet door and put the padlock back. After replacing the key on top of the refrigerator, I would climb back down onto the kitchen chair and, from there, down to the floor. Then I would slide the chair over to the table, go back into my bedroom with my sleeping grandfather, climb up on his chair and back into the crib. I had cookies inside the zipper of my footie pajamas and must have looked like a Teletubby. After eating those cookies, I'd go back to sleep.

My pre-dawn cookie raids were one big adventure on the farm. Gramp would wake up at about 9 a.m., pop me out of the crib, change my diaper and bring me out to the kitchen table. He'd make oatmeal or fix me some Cheerios and then he'd sit me down. While I was eating, we would talk. He usually drank his coffee, told me stories and sometimes recited poetry. Then he'd get me dressed, tie my shoes and boot me out of the house for the day. I would wait for him to come out to bring water to the chickens, and then I would walk down the path with him to collect the eggs. I was his helper.

People liked eggs. I brought eggs to school with me when I was older. Teachers bought the farm-fresh eggs and I would always ask if they wanted them delivered. On some nights, people would drive up to the farm to get their eggs. It was a great time in my life. I remember our having at some point to nip off the tips of the chickens' beaks. If they were going to be layers, they couldn't be eating their own eggs or pecking them too closely. They would crack the eggs if they did that. So I learned a lot about raising chickens, and it was definitely fun for a child.

As I got older, I had the paper route, I caddied and I also cooked in a restaurant at a golf club on Saturdays. Gramp was starting to age. I knew he was 61 years older than I. That meant someday I was going witness his demise.

Once I entered high school, Gramp and I had less and less time together. I certainly couldn't help with the chickens anymore. He was approaching his 80's. We used to like to watch Red Skelton on Tuesday nights and it was pretty good television. We also watched television together on Thursday nights and had a lot of fun doing that. We both loved the old *Dean Martin Show.*

There was a program about a detective named Harry O that we both enjoyed. While sitting together, we could talk with each other about pressing problems in my life and things that were on our minds. I was very fortunate in having Gramp pass down to me a wealth of experience and knowledge concerning the things that were really important in life.

The subject of nursing homes came up once or twice a year and Gramp always said he could never deal with a nursing home. We had a very large, extended family that included 22 cousins. That meant 22 grandchildren for Gramp, and it meant there was always something going on: a Christening, a First Communion, a Confirmation, birthdays and all kinds of Christmas dinners. There was constant growth and progress in our family, and everyone would talk about what they were doing at work or in school. It definitely kept him young, because he was involved with so many young people. That was especially true when the great-grandchildren began to arrive. Between the weddings, the Christenings, the birthdays and all of the holidays, it was truly a wonderful time.

Not surprisingly, Saint Patrick's Day was a huge holiday in my family. Sunday was church day, and Saturday was beans and franks night, while watching *The Lawrence Welk Show.* So our lives were pretty much planned. I think the fact Gramp did much of the cooking, a lot of the laundry and much of the mentoring in our family kept him very young, even though it was chaotic at times. I cannot imagine 10 people sitting down at the dinner table every night, but they say after the first six it doesn't really matter anyway. Making dinner for 10 people every day of the week must have been quite a chore. And then we had one of my aunts or uncles join us on Sunday. I still have the cherry caned chair where Gramp sat. It's a beautiful antique chair, and you can see it in my office at Kelly Financial when you come in to visit with me.

Gramp and I used to sit in that chair, in front of the picture window that overlooked about 15 acres of the farm, with a lane that led down to the main road. Hour after hour he would recite poems, sing me songs and tell me stories. Sometimes he would sit me in the chair, then get up to tap dance and sing the old Vaudeville songs. Two of his favorite poems were *The Village Blacksmith* and *In the Cool, Cool, Cool of the Evening.* Gramp could could sing patriotic songs and George M. Cohan songs. He also knew a lot of things about life. We spent so much time together, talking for a lot of it. He helped me learn how to save money. He was there for my graduation, and for every other important event in of my life.

Gramp was sure about one thing, and that one thing was he didn't want to be confined to a nursing home, ever. He was a big man and the strongest human being I've ever known. William has a lot of Gramp's characteristics. They are both very similar in their attitudes toward many things. My son is going to be a very big man, too. His chest, hands and feet are huge. They say size skips a generation.

As time went on, Mom and Dad retired from the phone company and the fire department, respectively. Gramp sold the farm. My folks bought a small condominium that overlooked the water. Things still looked pretty good. Gramp began to slip a little bit, but he could still get around and was doing well.

I had been working for a landscaping company when I found out I would be going away to school at the Air Force Technical Institute in Denver. Lo and behold, the landscaping company offered me a huge raise right before I was due to leave. I came home to let Gramp know, saying, "Look, I'm going to be able to stay here! They've offered me a tremendous raise. I'm going to have a lot of work this winter and I think I might even be able to start my own landscaping company."

Basically, I was telling him that we could stick together, that our team did not have to break up yet. He looked at me, almost in shock, and said, "There is no way you can stay here, because if you do, you're not going to get any type of education that you'll be needing to move ahead in life. Yes, you and I will have a great time for the next five to 10 years, but pretty soon I am going to be moving along and you will have to find something that's going to secure you." He told me that my path was pretty much determined, if I was going to learn, and it meant I was going away. The conversation ended with his saying, "You must do it." Although I was taken aback, I knew that's what had to happen. So off I went.

As time went by, Gramp began to fall and couldn't really maneuver as well as he used to. Since he was a big man, it was very difficult for my parents to lift him up. He wasn't injured when he fell, but he started to hit his head and lose his balance. He never lost his ability to think, reason or enjoy life, but he was just getting old. Pretty soon, the falls got worse. He fell one evening when my folks were away, so he had a bad night on the floor. It was decided that Gramp needed to go into the nursing home.

If you're an old Irish family, you have a lot of anticipation of gloom and doom when it comes to nursing homes, because it's inherent in our DNA that people will come and take our homes and force us to do things we fear. And that is something we have yet to overcome. So was it a good day for me? No, and Gramp was never the same. He left a family of eight children, 22 grandchildren and 11 great-grandchildren in order to re-establish his life in a nursing home.

He was put into a room with someone who had a totally different personality from his. They didn't get along and it was a rocky road for a while. His heart was so strong that I think he'd still be living today if things had gone right. He'd be 110, but he'd still be here. Unfortunately, dear reader, you learned in Chapter 3 how badly things ended for my Gramp, Timothy Murphy, in that nursing home.

Can you prevent that? I hope so. Is it going to happen to you? I don't think so. That's what happened to Gramp and that's what I keep in mind when I see people sitting across from me in my office. How are we going to help them? How are we going to keep something similar from happening in their lives? If you don't have a plan, you need to get one, because it's too late when you're in the ambulance and on your way to the nursing home. That's why we use a great tool called "forecasting" at our office, and that's why we think it's important for you to do the same thing. Regardless of your circumstances, you can benefit from planning. I have found good long-range planning produces great short-term results. Don't ask me why. It's a mindset. I think once you start doing the planning, the universe kind of looks at you and says, "He's making a plan and we've got to respect that and respond by aligning with his needs." So we want to make sure we keep what we have, grow it a little bit if we can, and pass on what's left. There are human lives behind every estate plan and every investment. What are we going to leave when we pass? What are we going to do while we're here to help others? These are the important issues.

So that, dear reader, is what life's all about. It's about planning. It's about family. It's about having fun. And it's about eventually and hopefully going to Heaven and meeting the people you love there.

CHAPTER NINETEEN

William Kelly Jr.

The people we love are the people for whom we plan. That never stops. Folks who come into my office have the same things in mind, almost to a person. They want to keep the assets they have, grow them a little bit, use a portion for themselves and pass on what's left. That planning process is called *preservation, growth and distribution.*

Our clients want to be able to fend for themselves, to enjoy life, to have some vacations and to increase their net worth. These are good aspirations. They also want to help their children and loved ones as they journey through life. This is part of the estate-planning process. In order to pass something along, you have to first preserve it. The estate-planning process is the topic of my book, *Senior Safe Money Strategies.* We need to keep that process in mind when we're investing, being sure we utilize models for capital preservation, asset allocation and growth, with possible income. We can then create a scenario in which that income is defined and projected, giving us goal posts, milestones and checkpoints to follow.

Having a son late in life has understandably made a big difference in how I think about my practice. I have changed many things, in anticipation that William may be running the company some day. This means I might have to extend my horizons by practicing for another 20 years. Having these goals has done a lot for me. They inspire me to do a better job every day by improving upon the things that occupy me on a regular basis. Those include my radio show. The radio show is different, as those of you who tune in realize. You never know what you're going to hear from the complex mind of Bill Kelly, but you can always be sure it will come straight from the heart. I mean what I say. And I definitely say what I mean, because my listeners and readers have no time for poking between the lines.

Our son is a miracle, of course. When Dr. Ali told us we were going to have a child, the first words out of his mouth were, "You're going to have a child and it's a miracle." He was right. William certainly has been a miracle. We are so fortunate and want you to know there *are* miracles in your life. We witness the miracle of life through our children and grandchildren. We also question death, and what happens to our loved ones when they pass on. It's a mystery of faith. Faith receives and love gives. It's also the story of people who plan for those who will survive them. We want you to keep that in mind at all times as part of your financial and estate planning.

For me, the miracle takes the form of tiny little William Kelly, who runs around the house, constantly smiling and always getting into something. William hasn't been sick one day of his life and always sleeps through the night. Great medical care gave us a wonderful start for this child. We are truly blessed and I know you, my friend, are experiencing blessings in your life in many different ways. I am pleased to be one of them, if and when I can be.

CHAPTER TWENTY
Cookies

Until now, I've never told anyone about my early-morning forays described in Chapter 18. That fact reveals a kind of solitary feeling that pervaded my life at that time. Being the youngest boy, I was always operating among all these big, huge people, perpetually looking at their knees and maneuvering around them to get what I needed.

I remember playing with a chemistry set when I was 7 or 8. It was the coolest thing, until I set my pajamas on fire with it. We stayed home from school because of a blizzard and I was looking for something to do. The chemistry set came with an alcohol burner, so I lit it and played with the flame. Next thing I knew, I had caught the cuff of my pajamas on fire. I ran through the house and got to my bed, grabbed the blankets and rolled myself up in them. I didn't get hurt, but I had burnt pajamas. That was my life.

On our Thursday-morning trip to the egg market, we'd buy a shinbone and make soup out of it with tomatoes. Can you imagine that? My mom would also buy something called Scotch ham, which is basically a half-inch-thick piece of sliced ham that she later fried. And she would buy a beef roast. Every Sunday we'd have roast beef or chicken.

Today, we're talking about possible food shortages. In the Bible, the Book of Timothy says, *The End Times are here when a man's wages for a day will equal the price of a loaf of bread.* So, people are debating about whether or not that's happening. Despite what is going on in the world, you need to take care of what is most important to you. If you ask people what is most important to them, they usually say that they want to preserve what they have. Do you want to keep what you now have? You probably haven't thought much about retirement in the last week, or maybe you are already retired. But in any event, you need to be focused on retaining what you have. That's essential.

I'd like to remind you again about the tools we have to help guide you, all available to you at no cost if you call our toll-free number: 1-888-800-1881. As mentioned in an earlier chapter, we also have my book, *Senior Safe Money Strategies,* a risk tolerance test and the National Senior Retirement Test Kit (NSRT). You will learn about your financial health and be able to determine where you stand in relation to the rest of the seniors in this country. Sometimes big things *do* come in little packages!

CHAPTER TWENTY-ONE
In My Room

On a morning in 1954, I woke up and looked through the screen in my crib to see Gramp's green khaki pants and wool plaid shirt with two button-down pockets still hanging on his chair. He was sitting on the end of the bed in his undershorts and a white tee-shirt. Gramp took a Camel cigarette from the wool shirt pocket and lit it, smoking it to the very end and then flicking the ashes into his hand. When he had taken the last puff, he spat into the palm of his hand and put the Camel out in the small pool of spit. Then he went into the bathroom and flushed it down the toilet, washed his hands and came back to get dressed and make breakfast. The day had begun.

1957

I could open the window of my new bedroom on the second floor and slide to the ground on a snow drift that reached the window sill. I had to sneak back into the house through the kitchen to repeat the act, unnoticed by my parents.

1959

I sat on the oak floor in my room with the new chemistry set my brother had gotten for Christmas. We were home from school for the day as a result of a blizzard. As I told you in the last chapter, I managed to catch my pajamas on fire, then extinguish it by using a blanket. The flames were gone, but the house smelled of fire and smoke. I had to go downstairs and get Gramp for help. He came up right away, more worried than angry, as usual.

1961

My new room was on the second floor and overlooked a large field. Two of my older brothers had left home, allowing for a realignment of quarters. I found our original television from the early '50s.

My folks were planning to bring it to the dump. During winter break, I dragged it up the stairs and crafted a primitive stand from cinder blocks and an old door. I brought all of the tubes to J&S Electronics and tested them, using money from my paper route to replace the bad tubes with brand new ones, purchased a cheap antenna and finally had my own television, a 20-inch Zenith, in my bedroom. That first night, with a feeling of total satisfaction, I watched *The Little Shop of Horrors* on *Creature Features*.

1962

On summer nights I would listen to programs from all over the country, on a crystal radio I had built. When radio waves from distant cities bounced off the ionosphere, then travelled thousands of miles back to a radio receiver, it was called "skip." Sometimes I would receive signals from New York. I remember watching *The Joe Pyne Show* late one Saturday night. Many times I read books and magazines under the bedspread, using a flashlight, far into the night and sometimes until daybreak.

1963

I cried inconsolably in bed the night my grandmother passed away. I cried even more, thinking about the fact that some day Gramp, too, would be gone. On the way back from the funeral, my cousin Donnie told me he was sorry I was so close to Gramp, as eventually I would have to bear the loss. He predicted it would be devastating. Ironically, Donnie passed before Gramp, on an "unsinkable" offshore oil rig during a hurricane, at age 29.

1963

I rushed home from school to turn on the television and watch a press conference with President Kennedy. Mom brought the ironing board into my room and she and Gramp watched the press conference with me. On the bedroom wall was a list I had made that included all the members of his Cabinet. Later that year, President Kennedy was killed. I cried all through the night. I begged God to reverse it and to take me in his place, so he could return to the nation and his family.

1970

Gramp had become ill and I spent the first night of my life at the house without him. He was at the hospital. I lay in bed all night and stared at the ceiling until daybreak.

1975

It was my last night at home. I was heading out for parts unknown. The "team" was breaking up and I did not have the wherewithal to realize it until the morning. During the next 30 years, I didn't return for any length of time.

CHAPTER TWENTY-TWO
School Days, Then and Now

I n 2009, I was reading an article about a young lady who was gang-raped in Richmond, California. The incident took place outside a high school dance and lasted several hours. It was absolutely horrible and, to my knowledge, there was no reason for this to happen. The young woman had not said or done anything to provoke it.

The administration held a school assembly at which students who were affected by the incident could talk and begin the healing process. A female student spoke into a microphone in front of the group, bemoaning the fact they had only four police officers at the dance. In her opinion, that was not enough to control the crowd. She further stated there were only nine police officers assigned to the school.

Although I sympathized with her feelings, I was simultaneously thinking, "*Only* nine police officers at the school? I must be from another planet! Why in God's name do they need *nine* police officers at a high school in California? Why aren't town officials doing something to put a stop to this and make things right?"

When I was a kid, we had five or six hundred students, and we had Uncle Jessie. That's who we had. You remember Uncle Jessie from Chapter 2. If you vomited, Uncle Jessie would come in with the red powder and throw it on the floor. That's what he did. And kids weren't stabbing each other there.

We also had Mrs. Carol. If you were in trouble, Uncle Jessie would come to your classroom and say, "You have to go see Mrs. Carol." When you got home, your parents had a slip saying you had seen Mrs. Carol, with a suggestion to please call the school. You got whacked by your parents and they wanted to know why you had disobeyed at school and why you had not followed the rules.

There was very little chance we would be raped, stabbed, beaten to death or clubbed with a pole. We weren't going to have six kids beating us up for a seat on the bus while someone else made a video of it. We all knew our driver and nobody made fun of him or gave him a bad time. At the beginning of the year, the students talked about which bus and driver they were going to get.

Suddenly, we are in a future that has gone terribly awry. We are in a place where we have no clue what's up and what's down and are witnessing a generation who have no respect for themselves, for each other or for persons in authority.

CHAPTER TWENTY-THREE
How to Tell You Are in a Family

Most people want to know things are going to work out in life, so they can enjoy their down time and take care of the people they love. And whom do they love? The people they've always loved. Whom do they want to help? Whom do you want to help? You want to help the very same people you have helped your entire life, your family and loved ones. Family is everything. Everything.

Don't ask me why I was chosen to be one of those people who talks about the joys of family life. I mean, I was a miserable human being, really. I didn't know how to have a family. But I soon discovered evidence that I am an integral part of a family. First of all, I have almost no hair, but everybody steals my hairbrush. That means I'm in a family. What else? I have no hair and buy my own cream rinse at Stop & Shop, the fructose kind that's green. It's like, man, I don't have lots of hair but I'm going to feel good in the morning when I put this cream rinse on my hair. I'm going to smell like a glade in the everglades. So I'm in the shower, all 220 pounds of me, and I'm brushing my teeth at the same time because I'm in a hurry.

I reach for the cream rinse and it's not there. Do you know what that means? If you're single and you reach for that cream rinse, it's going to be there. But if you have a family of people with thick hair, it's not. I don't know who has the most hair per square inch, but we could win an Olympic hair thickness contest in our house.

So I was relaxing in a nice hot shower and now I have to get out in the cold air, stick my head around the corner, dripping on the rug, and yell loudly enough to be heard all over the house because everybody's doing his own thing in the morning. "Where's my cream rinse?" Then a little person comes in and says, "Oh, I borrowed it." And I respond to him, "Well, can I get it back? I really like my cream rinse."

"Oh sure, Pop." So I get my cream rinse back. That means I'm in a family, because a single person doesn't go through that. When you're single everything is lined up, from shaving brush to floss. But that's not family life, unless you live in some kind of family of which I am unaware.

I drive 45 minutes to get home from the office, talking on the phone to get more work done. I want to get home and watch *The O'Reilly Factor*. It comes on at 8 p.m., so I want to get that thing set up. I walk into the living room and there are people using Wii and jogging on platforms through virtual woods with little fake animals. I begin with, "You know what? I *really* want to watch Bill O'Reilly." They look at me and say, "Oh, we're jogging on the Wii." So I go into the bedroom to eat dinner and watch O'Reilly on the little 12-inch television. That's how I know I'm in a family.

Now if you're single, you come home to an automatic light dimmer and you engage it. The curtains pull back and your big-screen television flashes on. There's O'Reilly and you have him TiVoed for a week. I go to my TiVo, dear reader, and how much is left on it? About eight percent. I'm trying to record a football game because I want to take the family out on Sunday, but there is not enough room on my TiVo. Instead, there are 12

Hannah Montana episodes and 15 episodes each of *Peep* and *Scooby-Doo*. My wife, Kelly, has stashed her soaps on there, for another 20 percent. So that's what's on the TiVo, and it means I'm not going to be able to TiVo the football game. That incident led to a big family meeting. I said, "Look, we're going to divide the TiVo. There are four of us here, so we each get 20 percent and there's another 20 percent storage that's optional, so all the family can share that."

All of a sudden, we're having a big fight over the TiVo space. Why? "I've got to have *Hannah Montana*!" We also record a show called *Full House*, on at just about every time of the day. Remember how we could always watch the *I Love Lucy* reruns? They were always on somewhere. Well, so is *Full House*, but we still have to record it.

And that's how you can tell you're in a family. Having a family and loving the people you're with is one of the greatest joys in life. But I will be at my children's houses someday and I will take over their living room or den. I don't know what the computers are going to look like in the future, but I'm going to take them over. I'm going to be there with my suitcase one night and my son or daughter will answer the door and the conversation will go something like this:

"It's Pop. What's he doing?"

"I'm moving in."

"What do you mean?"

"I'm moving into your den and I want the computer, I want the remote and I want the Wii."

And then they'll say, "Wow, we have a family, don't we?"

CHAPTER TWENTY-FOUR
School Clothes

What did I do on the anniversary of Reverend King's speech? I had called the Martin Luther King Center, in Newport, the week before and asked the director if she had any families who needed school clothes.

"Do I have any families who need shoes or school clothes? Everybody does," she said. I told her I wanted her to bring every child she could to meet me at Old Navy at 11 a.m. on Sunday. "Well," she said, "I think they're going to show up. They don't trust a lot of people, but we know you. I'm going to put out a flyer." And I blessed the idea with my hearty approval.

We called the Center a few days before Sunday. It sounded as if we would have a good turnout, so I called the manager at Old Navy and told her I wanted everyone to have two tee-shirts and a jacket. "I want them to have two pairs of pants or shorts, whatever they want for school, whatever's appropriate."

Kelly and my two children, Mary Madeline and William, had gone to Georgia to be with her folks, so I was alone on Sunday. For some reason I started thinking the meeting was at noon, and I was getting ready to leave. It was actually 11:10 a.m..

I went over to the counter in my house and picked up the flyer they had faxed me: **Kelly Financial. Meet at Old Navy. 11:00 a.m. Sponsoring a school clothing drive.** *Great. I'm late. They're going to get to the store and think,"This guy's full of it."*

I called the manager to say I was on my way. I got there about 11:35, walked in and found her. When asked if the people from the Center were there, she responded there were about 30 of them, and they were all over the store. So I went back to the children's clothing area. A group of people were there and one of them looked at me. I asked if they were from the Center and she replied they were. I said, "Great! How's it going?" They all said that it was going well, but one of the ladies came up to me and asked if she could trade a shirt for some socks and underwear. I don't get into the details of dressing kids, but every mother knows clean socks and underwear are pretty basic items. I realized I had forgotten something, so I said, "Yes, but don't trade anything. You need socks and underwear? Get socks and underwear." Then I announced, "If anyone wants socks and underwear, get them."

And so I met and shook the hand of every child and parent. They seemed really pleased with that. I wanted to let them know that I meant this, and there was no sacrifice of dignity in their accepting the clothing. I told them the story of my childhood and that as a child I didn't always have a lot of new clothes. There were seven kids and that meant a lot of hand-me-downs, but I loved having an outfit that was new on the first day of school.

That feeling would last, dear reader, and I looked forward to it. "What am I going to wear the first day of school?" We didn't have new outfits for the first 10 days of school, but everyone dwells on that first day. We want to look a certain way. All I know is I'd be up the night before, ironing my shirt just right with Niagara spray starch.

Another lady approached me, quite embarrassed, and told me she couldn't bring her daughter because the child was sick. I replied her daughter's presence wasn't necessary at all "Get the child the clothes she needs." After about a half-hour, everyone seemed to be ready. I went up to the cash registers with three credit cards, handed them over and then signed the slips as everyone checked out. At one point, I remembered Bank of America would probably shut the card down because of the number of transactions. So I called and told the CSR what I was up to at Old Navy and we got that all squared away.

The people from the Center made three lines at the checkout counter, and received their clothes. People were hugging me. Women were crying and thanking me. I received letters of gratitude in the mail. There was one from a woman whose son was growing so fast, she had to put clothes on layaway:

Bill, I want to thank you again for your kindness and your generosity. I can't tell you how much you've helped me, just by helping my son. It has been a very difficult year for me personally, and I have tried to help my 6-year-old by insulating him from what was happening as much as possible. In spite of that, he notices the little things like fewer toys and less expensive amenities. I'm grateful he didn't have to know what it's like to not have a new outfit for school again this year. I tried getting something each pay period, but with his recent growth spurt, some things are already too small. I could go on and on, but I really just want to thank you, and I wish you and your family every possible goodness and blessing.

Sincerely, Jackie.

So, you see, we can help people, one by one. It can work on a small scale and it can work on a large scale. Why did I do it? Because I wanted to pass on the feeling of joy I had in going back to school with a new outfit. Some of these people were minorities. Some of them were Irish. That has no bearing. They were kids in a situation not of their making. None of it was their fault. The circumstances had befallen their parents. So we have to learn to help each other. We're good people, my friend. Don't let anyone tell you we're not, because we are, and we help each other. That's what we do. That's how we're going to get out of the fix we're in. We're going to help one another.

CHAPTER TWENTY-FIVE
Getting a Break

Does welfare work? I can give you some examples that prove it does. How about if I take you back to my own experience? You are probably thinking, *Bill Kelly on Welfare? Right!* Well, let me tell you about it.

As mentioned earlier in the book, I graduated from high school an honor student. I also appeared in *Who's Who Among American High School Students*, won the National Youth Leadership Award, was student council president and a Merit Scholar. I also told you of my desire to learn about working with electronics. My plan was to take a year off from school, and then go back to further my education and become an engineer.

A shoo-in, right? Wrong. Many, many things got in the way. My first real job out of school was hauling trash for a foundation that restored homes built before 1800 and named, aptly enough, the Restoration Foundation. Generally, the trash man would be laid off for the winter so I figured I would end up collecting unemployment for a while.

I was talking to Gramp one day and mentioned that I was expecting to be unemployed that winter and wasn't sure where I wanted to go to school. He said, "Well, go down to the unemployment office and see Mary Hackett. She might offer something a little better than unemployment." This was my first political favor, because I had driven for the Democrats for two years since I had gotten my license. I had always helped out at the polls whenever I could, and my parents were staunch Irish Catholic Democrats. My mother held teas and other gatherings in her living room.

I went down to the unemployment office and spoke with Mary Hackett, who said, "There's a program that will send you to electronics school." Back then, New England Institute of Technology was nowhere nearly as well formed as it is now. It was just a small school in Providence. Mary then said, "What we're going to do is pay you $80 a week while you go to New England Tech, and then when you're done, we will place you somewhere for employment." She added, "But if you can find an employer to sponsor you and to state they will hire you when you leave New England Tech, you can have this scholarship." They were going to pay the tuition *and* pay me $80 a week to go to school. I told her that sounded like a great deal."

I went to one of the electronics firms in Providence and told them what I wanted to do. They said they would write me a letter when I graduated and during the summer I could come and work for them. But it was a year-round school. So I set everything up: I went to Radio Shack and got some electronics kits, then borrowed books from the library. I experimented and made all kinds of devices in my bedroom, really learning about electronic circuitry in the process.

In the middle of the summer, when I visited New England Tech, they showed me what I would be doing. I got a couple of the textbooks so I could start studying early. My bedroom looked like some kind of laboratory. Then Dad met an Air Force recruiter at a Knights of Columbus meeting. The recruiter said, "They're looking for people who want to learn computer science. They'll teach you everything you to need to know, but you have to pass an aptitude test." When he told me about it, I said I wanted to give it a shot!

I told the Air Force recruiter, Sergeant Fry, that I had a full scholarship to learn electronics and asked him if he had anything better. He said, "Yes, the F-15." That was 35 years ago and the plane was brand new. He continued, "The F-15 is going to be completely computer-tested. We will put you in school for a year and a half, but you'll have to sign up for six years. We'll get you at least an Associate's Degree and help you with some other tuition. We need people, so if you can pass this aptitude test, we'll enroll you in the school." I told him I hadn't really started at New England Tech, but had been studying like crazy, so I would go ahead and take the test.

I scored a 98 in electronics. Sergeant Fry said, "I think you can get this, but are you willing to take that risk? You'll have to sign up for a six-year stay, but if you do, we'll guarantee you an advanced technical school in Denver." So I did it. John, my fellow trash truck driver, was very interested in electronics. I told him I wasn't going to take the scholarship to New England Tech and suggested we go to the unemployment office to see if he could have it.

We went and spoke to Mrs. Hackett. I told her I had been accepted to a two-year school at the Air Force Technical Center in Denver and I really wanted to pursue that. Later on, John got accepted and took my place at New England Tech.

I never took the welfare, did I? But I was prepared to. The government would have been giving me money while I was going to school and not working. So I went to school in Denver and learned how to do computerized testing of F-15 aircraft, the first of its type. They sent me all over the world. For six years, I was constantly in school and made fabulous money when I got out. That delayed my going back to college even more. On my first job out of the Air Force, I was earning well in excess of $100,000, incredibly enough. It was totally worth the struggle, believe me.

That first meeting with Mary Hackett was a favor, I guess. Anyone can know anyone else through six degrees of separation. And that's all you need. So I had an assisted launch. Then again, I ended up knowing I had that help and took a further little jump off the perch to try to better myself. I knew my baseline was going to be attending New England Tech and having a job in electronics technology. Knowing that made me feel a lot better. But I ended up having a fabulous technical education and a fabulous job. I traveled the world, helped to defend the country and then put on my civilian hat again. That journey was a great 10-year period in my life.

I was single and didn't have my own family then. But I was not in despair, nor was I asking the government to take care of my entire life and do everything for me. I just needed a little bit of a boost, which I got. And it dramatically changed my life at that time. A helping hand often seems to work better than just giving someone total welfare. It's that old "hand up instead of a handout."

Now you might be disadvantaged and wondering how you can get a helping hand. You might live in a housing project and find it difficult to feed your family. Well, there are ways to get help and people to help you. But figuring out a good way to game the system for the next 30 years isn't the answer.

I mentioned my family lived in housing projects before we bought Bailey Brook Farm, with the help of Gramps. My whole family moved from Providence to a housing project known as Tonomy Hill, in Newport. It was a mix of nationalities back then, but mostly Irish and Italian. We would visit my grandmother at Tonomy Hill. To me, she lived in a museum. She kept the apartment immaculate and made it wonderful to look at, with her knick-knacks and beautiful curtains. The yards were kept up and the premises were kept clean.

My grandmother was 65 and the neighborhood bully was named Bobby Brooks. If he came through her yard and left a gum wrapper, my grandmother would yell at him. Picture someone who looked like the Fonz, right? If the Fonz got his character from someone, it was this guy Bobby Brooks. So here's a 65-year-old Italian lady in an open bedroom window, pointing a finger and yelling at a hoodlum. "Bobby Brooks, if you don't pick that gum wrapper up, I'm coming down there. And if I come down there, you're not going to like it. I'm going to call your mother before I go down there, and I know what she's going to tell me. She's going to tell me to do whatever I need to do." So that was my grandmother. And Bobby Brooks, the neighborhood hoodlum, would look up and say, "Okay, Mrs. Murphy. I'll get the wrapper. Sorry about that. I'm outta here." He was the toughest kid I knew. Back then, when you heard an adult yelling at you from a window, you listened. But things have changed a lot since then.

We didn't know we were poor and we didn't know my grandmother was poor. We didn't think of it as a project. To us, she lived at 19 Cowie Street. About 20 years ago I was driving through that neighborhood and they were tearing it apart again. It's been redeveloped four different times in 40 years, typical with public housing. I wondered if 19 Cowie Street was still there, so I went back. The door was open and off its hinges. The whole street was being redone.

I walked into the apartment and what a shock! It was tiny. The kitchen was 10 x 10, the living room was probably 10 x 15 and there was a set of stairs leading to the top floor, where there were two bedrooms. One was probably 10 x 12 and the other was probably 12 x 12. There also was a bathroom.

A feeling of claustrophobia took hold. Those stairs used to gleam. When you went to Grandma's house, you dusted before you went to bed at night. When you got up in the morning, after breakfast, you cleaned the stairs with Pledge. That's what happened at Grandma's house. The beds were made perfectly. Everything was neat and orderly, all in public housing.

My uncles lived at Tonomy Hill, too, in the house next door to ours. The funny thing is, they would save some money, then they would move out and buy a starter home. That's what they did. As you know, Mom worked for the phone company and Dad was a fireman. He also worked at a hardware store. So those were the three jobs I spoke of earlier in the book. Mom sold real estate once in a while because she had a knack for it. Then, suddenly and with the help of Gramp, they bought Bailey Brook Farm.

And that was the beginning of the next phase of our lives. They were out of the projects. We didn't call them that then, but would certainly call them that now. One day we were living in Tonomy Hill. The next day, we had a big farm with thousands of chickens, and everyone was happy. My uncles got work in hardware stores. My Uncle Tom started working at Raytheon and got put through radio school. Just imagine that. He began working at Raytheon and all of a sudden found a great career!

Did we have an advantage because our skin color was white? I don't know. But I'll tell you what advantage we *did* have. If we didn't have a job, it didn't go over well at the dinner table in my family. At the ripe old age of 9, we were expected to work.

We could deliver a newspaper, we could caddy, we could mow lawns or we could shovel snow. I don't know what has happened since then. When my daughter Mary Madeline was 12, I couldn't imagine telling her to go out to work. But now she works our seminars and sometimes is in the office. She enjoys greeting people. There are things that kids can do.

There was a path to improvement for me, a path that went onward and upward. I'm sure there's also a way out for others today. However, I don't think the way out is by "fundamentally transforming" our government into a quasi-Communist and bloated bureaucracy in which we have to share the wealth with everyone. We weren't told anyone was going to share his or her wealth with us when we were growing up. We were told we had to get a job. I seriously believe there's some sort of disconnect these days.

CHAPTER TWENTY-SIX

What We Didn't Have

The most incredible thing to ponder is what I had and did not have growing up. When I take William to school, we enter through a secure glass partition, then walk to an office and sign him in. At the end of his day, we pick him up and bring him home. That's our weekday routine with William.

When I entered first grade, we walked three-quarters of a mile down the lane and got on a yellow bus with a driver nicknamed Dogface. I don't know why that was his nickname. It was a terrible thing. The kids in the back of the bus would try to get Dogface to stop the bus and run back there to discipline them. They dared him to do that. There were some slightly risqué things going on in first and second grade. However, if Dogface turned those kids in, they were in deep trouble, both at school and at home.

Our parents had so much on their family plate. We didn't even have seat belts in our car. Imagine that? There was no law requiring them. I told you earlier about that strap on the bench seat, the five kids pulling on the rope across the seats and my mother's very educated "backhander." There was no air conditioning in either our car or our home. As a matter of fact, half the time we had no heat.

To summarize earlier chapters, one bathroom for 10 people and three bedrooms for five (eventually, seven) kids. My parents had their own bedroom on the first floor and Gramp and

I had ours on the first floor. The fact I bunked with Gramp was good for me, logistically, because I could get to the cupboards and indulge my cookie addiction without having to go down the stairs from the second floor. If I slept on the second floor, the game would be up, because the stairs made so much noise. So bunking with Gramp was okay by me.

We didn't have cell phones, of course. We had a two-party phone, and we did indeed listen to that second party whenever we could. Being curious children, we wanted to know what was going on at our neighbor's house. Somewhere along the way, the phone company decided to revamp the location of the second party. Since it wasn't always a neighbor after that, it wasn't as much fun listening in. Our phone number was 401-846-2484 and I got that number when I picked up a VoIP account six years ago. My folks have moved on to Heaven, but that number was available, so I have it. Every once in a while, someone from the past calls it and I'm pleased to be able to speak with them. That number has been in my family since 1938, I believe.

We had the same Mixmaster from the time I was born to the time I went into the Air Force. That Mixmaster and three stainless steel bowls served my mother well. Now people buy food processors, blenders, shredders, cutters—all manner of devices for the kitchen. We had the same potato masher my entire life. You know, the one with the handle and all the holes in the stainless steel part that mashed the potatoes? Think about that. Back then things were made in the United States, not China, so they lasted a lifetime with no problem (and no lead in the metal either). Product integrity.

So that's what we had. What didn't we have? We didn't have a skin specialist, a heart specialist and a bladder specialist. We had one doctor, Dr. Bestoso, and he charged us two dollars to see him. Dr. Bestoso would always be smoking a Pall Mall cigarette. I'd be sitting there looking at him and he'd be looking at me, asking what's wrong. My mother would say, "He's got the croup!" Everyone had the croup back then. You would cough your lungs out, because with our finicky heating system, we would freeze half to death much of the time. The solution was always the same. We'd first get a prescription for Cheracol and then we'd take Luden's or Smith Brothers cough drops. At night we'd go to bed with a sock that had been filled with salt and heated in the oven. We got one vaccination, for smallpox. Everyone got measles and everyone got chickenpox, but we got through it.

From third grade on, we all ironed our own clothing. If we didn't, we had wrinkled clothing. We knew how to use spray starch, which was actually a new invention back then. In the dining room, there would be a line of kids ironing their shirts. We ate home-cooked meals and we had a consistent menu. We probably had a 10-meal rotation for my entire life, so there was not a lot of change.

I think we're on our third set of laptops at my house these days. My daughter, Mary Madeline, has her third cell phone in six years. Every time I replace my cell phone, I can predict what's going to happen. The people in my house are going to see it, but they're not going to ask for it. They're just going to look at it for a few months. Then they're going to talk about how nice it is, and say, "Gee, I wish I had this feature on my cell phone, because if I did, Pop, I'd be able to get in touch with you more quickly." This is an amazing, amazing time. Technology is moving so fast and kids are growing up so fast (maybe too fast). The technological aspect of living in the 21st century is incredible. But as a nation, I think we're regressing. We're abandoning our quest for knowledge of outer space and the moon because we're going broke. Our ability to dream is also being thwarted.

Art Williams is one of the motivational speakers I admire. He says, "Just do it and stop talking!" It's a pretty good way to look at things. Do the best you can, do all you can whenever you can and that will take you a long way toward success. It's not a guaranteed formula, but it certainly is a good way to start. Art Williams is a brilliant man and he follows the Boy Scout Code, I can tell you. He is trustworthy, loyal and reverent, and he has given hundreds of millions of dollars to Christian causes.

Art was a football coach who wanted to save $35,000 in order to augment his teacher's pension, and he ended up selling about $100 billion worth of term life insurance. I think he did it in one year, his best year. So, Art Williams formed an insurance company that is now Primerica. He was given the freedom to dream. But we're suffocating the ability of this generation to dream. It's a mistake to limit people. If we have kids waiting for a handout from the government, instead of being self-reliant, and if they don't learn it's okay to win (or lose) in competitions, they will never learn to strive. We should embrace exceptionalism, rather than treat it like a dirty word. We don't want to bully kids or hurt them physically, but we most certainly want them to know that competition can be a great tool.

One of the greatest experiences of my life was winning a mile race, because I'd never run it before and I thought it was impossible. I did it because our track team needed someone to fill in for the fellow who usually ran it. I was a sprinter, but I was able to win a mile race in high school only through the grace of God. Do you know what inspired me while I was running that race? I was thinking about Bill Russell the entire time, and how he overcame such adversity when he was matched up against the great basketball centers of his day, guys such as Wilt Chamberlain and Nate Thurmond. He always found a way to outsmart them and he didn't have to score to win. He knew if he was a genius on defense, he could be a Hall of Fame player and a champion, which he is to this day.

So kids need to be able to dream. Kids need to know that if they have a dream, there's a chance for it to happen in their lives. They need that. If the government takes over all medical care in our country and tries to regulate it the way they are regulating every other program in their inflated bureacracy, like every other program in their inflated bureacracy, it will be a mess. It doesn't mean I'm a racist or don't want others to have medical care. It means we have to figure out a better way to do it. We have to do it in the private sector and person-to-person. Once the government gets in, it's like the camel's nose under the tent. You cannot get rid of them. Everybody has a little piece of the healthcare pie, so to speak, and everyone has to be responsible for the part they are chewing on, dear reader.

We didn't have a school psychologist and we didn't have a policeman to guard the school. I was shocked to find out most middle schools have a police officer nowadays. Some large high schools have three or four police officers assigned to them. We never had such a thing. We had only Uncle Jessie. We didn't seem to have as many autistic children as we have nowadays. It's a problem. I hope we can find the reason for the increasing number of cases we see of this. We didn't have Ritalin, the modern-day babysitter in overcrowded classrooms, or any kind of medication for Attention Deficit Disorder. Back then, children were labeled "very active," rather than ADD or ADHD.

We basically were forced to be disciplined. I don't want to intimate in any way, shape or form that I think discipline can overcome a disability. Either we didn't actually have a disability, or it wasn't as apparent if we did have it. Classroom sizes were smaller and the teacher had more control over the kids.

We knew no one who had Alzheimer's, although one of our aunts eventually had a confirmed diagnosis of the disease. It was called dementia back then. Now we're seeing case, after case, after case. Some people assign blame to aluminum cookware or statin drugs. Recent research has proven our penchant for substituting chemicals for saturated fats, via imitation this and imitation that, has resulted in the burgeoning cases of Alzheimer's. Saturated fats, in moderation, are absolutely necessary for both heart health and brain health. Back then, we ate butter, bacon and pot roast. And things like Alzheimer's just didn't exist, except for the isolated case here and there.

It was rare for us to miss a day of school. We didn't have counselors until we got to high school, and then we were assigned a guidance counselor. For me, it was Mrs. Maynard and she handled about 30 of us in our class. She probably had a caseload of 120 kids, but it was always great to speak with her. I always felt special and could tell she loved education.

So the world has turned upside down. There was a song entitled, *The World Turned Upside Down,* that was played during the British surrender march at Yorktown. I think that is what has happened and it's playing out in the markets. We all need to pay attention to this as we move forward.

America is a great country. It was once and will be again a shining star on the face of Earth. But right now, the star is a little dim and more than a little tarnished. We have to get to work, and hard work is what we do best. I wish the people in Washington were telling us this. We can tell each other for now, and later on they'll catch on. If we agree to work hard, memories of the goodness of this country will come floating back. They will present themselves again and we will enjoy a plentiful and tolerant spirit, one in which we feel complete, successful and content as a nation. How's that for an image to carry to bed with you tonight, my friend?

CHAPTER TWENTY-SEVEN
The Farm in Spring

What would be happening at the farm in spring? We would be counting the days until school ended and thinking, sixteen days and a wake up! That means there are 17 days to go, but the last day we wake up for school is probably going to be a half-day, and then we are finished. So we might as well just pretend the last full day doesn't exist. See? Sixteen days and a wake up!

I would be getting my transistors in order. The little 9-volt batteries were 29 cents, the transistor was $1.99 and there was a little earpiece you needed to buy. If I put the transistor in my pocket and ran the earplug up my sleeve, I could lean on my hand and listen to the Red Sox while my teacher, Mrs. Lane, was exploring mathematics. (You had to raise your hand a lot, so the teacher wouldn't catch on.) Generally, she would repeat a question anyway, and I would answer and look like a star. But don't tell your children that. It's bad.

In early summer, all the baby chicks were out of their brooder coop, hopping around, and were about three or four inches tall. We started to be on the lookout for those predators I mentioned. We'd fix up all the holes in the chicken-wire fencing. Chicken wire could be used for almost anything. We could put other material over the chicken wire if a screen broke. We could make temporary forts using chicken wire. We could build up the grass on the backside of a stone wall, and make the sides of a fort or a pirate ship. We could make darned near anything with chicken wire.

My brother crashed our car one of those summers. It was probably a '49 or '52 Dodge. The front grille was gone, so Dad fillled the void with chicken wire. I thought it must have had something to do with the airflow, but never really asked him about it. In high school physics class, there was something that reminded me of that time, and I asked the teacher what he thought the purpose of the chicken wire was. He had no idea, so I figured I would ask my dad when I got home and I did, while we were eating dinner. He told me he didn't like the blank spot where the grille used to be. He used the chicken wire, "so that it will look like something's there." I had spent all those years trying to interpret his actions, and in the final analysis, it had been done for cosmetic purposes only. No one would drive around in a Dodge with a gaping hole in front of the radiator. The little mysteries you have in a family.

My older brother started to sell encyclopedias at one point. My parents bought a set, of course, and received a Webster's dictionary with it. That dictionary was about a foot tall and had screws in the spine. The cover was similar to leather and was very, very stiff. We used to stand on it at the front window and see cars a mile away coming down the lane. Their lights bobbed up and down on the rocky road, telling us how far away the car was, so we could gauge when our folks were coming home. Once they were spotted, we would have about two minutes to clean. Sometimes we had to lock the back door to give ourselves an extra minute. Things are so different now. We have cell phones, tracking devices and driveway alarms.

I know you enjoy the stories of years ago. It was an amazing time, wasn't it? I also know the values of people who are able to retire successfully. I believe they have good solid values, because solid character values often translate into solid investment values. I think that's important.

In *Senior Safe Money Strategies*, you'll read some of my views that have developed in the 18 years since I received my first license to handle finance. It has been an incredible journey. At Kelly Financial, we love to meet people. We have some brunches scheduled in the coming months at both Café Escadrille and Lombardo's. You can meet me and my staff and get to know us.

And don't forget the National Senior Retirement Test (NSRT), to help you assess where you stand among your peers, and to get an idea of what you need to do. Thousands have taken that test. People always ask me, "Where do I stand in relation to other people my age?" Generally, I tell them they're in good standing if they are standing there with me.

Again, the *Will & Trust Workbook* is available if you call in. We also have a booklet published by the Secretary of the Commonwealth that gives you information on the various government departments and how they can help you. It's a great resource that lists all the departments in Massachusetts that could possibly have anything to do with your retirement. So call me at 1-888-800-1881 and ask for the booklet by William Francis Galvin,. He is an admirable person who has done a lot for Massachusetts that you will never hear about, primarily because he doesn't make many commercials about himself. It's amazing how much Galvin has done.

I don't think we have to be at each other's throats, dear reader. My key issue is abortion, and everyone knows it. But since I'm not a woman, I have to tread carefully. The pace at which abortions are being performed frightens me. I would do anything to help someone avoid an abortion if they felt they needed to do it for financial reasons. In fact, I have done so. Other than that, the political parties are pretty much the same. The Democrats tax and spend, and the Republicans cut taxes and spend. Neither party has impressed me with anything that's happened in Washington this year.

So much for politics. I can't really get into it. You see your fortunes being toyed with, and you wonder. Basically, I have to stick to my knitting here, my friend. And that means telling you stories about my life at Bailey Brook Farm. Stay tuned for the next installment.

CHAPTER TWENTY-EIGHT

Gertrude T. Kelly

O ne of my mother's great gifts to all of her children was the air of grace and beauty that she brought to many, many special occasions. Today, the day she is laid to rest, Mom has once again shared her gift with us.

In my mind, Mom is linked to The Blessed Virgin. It is difficult for me to think of one without the other. As a child I saw prayers to Mary, taped to a window and viewed though tree limbs stripped by autumn's chill. They symbolized certainty, allowing me to know in my heart Mom was praying for us all.

On the way to her service, I had the radio on. The words of the Beatles' song, *Let It Be*, were both relevant and comforting. *When I find myself in times of trouble, Mother Mary comes to me, speaking words of wisdom, let it be!* Today, Mom surely knows about something that remains a mystery to all of us seated here in this church.

With her final breath so resembling the first breath of my own son, one that William breathed with me eight years ago, I am convinced Mom's healing cycle has come full circle. Ours continues on today, as we sit here in church on a misty spring morning, in a row of silent spring days. We gather here in faith. Faith receives and love gives.

Mother's children were blessed with remarkable talent and ability. My brother Richard has an unending commitment to perseverance, creating businesses and enterprises where none existed before. My brother Walter has an unwavering faith in the promises of Jesus Christ and a large capacity for discipline and hard work, resulting in great success. Michael has fostered a beautiful family and was steadfast in his oath that my parents would never enter a nursing home in their declining years. Nancy is kind to all people, always has time to help others and worked diligently and consistently for years with Michael in order to care for my parents and see to all their personal needs and their dignity as their health ebbed in later years.

Oftentimes I would come home to find Dad reading the paper. Once I noticed him perusing the obituaries and asked him what he was reading. He said, "I am reading a list of the names of people who have quit smoking!"

My father's humor was always a source of comfort to us all. It was ballast to even out our journey on the ship of life. A tail wind for our travel, it eased us through waters often choppy, sometimes treacherous and always challenging.

Mom's first exposure to Dad's sense of humor occurred on the evening they met. He was a waiter in a small Providence café. Mom was sitting in a booth, waiting for her evening's escort. After almost an hour he still hadn't shown up. Dad, the ever-efficient waiter, offered to buy Mom a coke (five cents back then).

He then told Mom he would be happy to escort her to the movies after his shift and they could have just as good a time. Mom agreed, with one condition. She said, "I will go with you as long as you are not Walter Kelly. I have heard a lot about him and all the girls say he is too much of a ladies' man for someone like me to date!" Dad assured Mom he definitely was not Walter Kelly!

Well, it is a little known fact that Walter J. Kelly Sr. became Jimmy Higgins for that first night of their life together. Mom managed to survive 68 years of Dad's humor thereafter.

Not one single time did Mom ever take the easy route in life. Born weighing two pounds in 1917, she remained a medical miracle the rest of her life. She spent her first months of life in a dresser drawer, confined to a small room with a kerosene heater adjusted to keep the temperature a constant 90 degrees. Mom must have inwardly grown to love the crowded conditions the dresser drawer afforded her because, later in life, she added two foster children, John and Richie, to her family of five children at Bailey Brook Farm. Adding Gramp to the mixture, there were 10 of us at the dinner table every Sunday. People often remarked on how quickly Dad would eat his meals. I have the same bad habit, probably an ingrained survival instinct learned long ago at that table of 10.

Ten at the dinner table was not adequate for Mom. Sunday dinners were opportunities for her to welcome her brothers, sisters, nieces, nephews and grandchildren to the table. The only real rule we had at our dinner table was this: There was always room for at least one more person.

Buster Brown shoes, the Fuller Brush man, the Spiegel Catalog, Mason's Furniture, Waldron's, the Puritan Shop, the Outlet Company, Shepard's and The Newport Youth Center all provided Mom with moments to display her impeccable taste in clothing and accessories and her ability to bring out the best in us through "dressing up."

I'm reminded of Mom's taste in Cindy Lauper's popular song, *True Colors*. She sings, *I see your true colors shining through, like a rainbow*. Mom would select clothing with hues and fabric that best reflected our true inner colors. Her true inner colors were revealed to the world through her sense of style. She could always surprise and delight us by looking her best at special occasions. Beautiful hands, almost sculpted from marble, perfect nails and the noble set of her chin reflected both inner and outer beauty. A calmness in her eye assured us she was ever centered, despite the chaos created by a mushrooming family of seven children.

Hard work was important to Mom. Being employed and staying productive were her passport to the terrain traversed by the fortunate and content. She sincerely felt her job as a telephone operator and my father's as a fireman were vital to the community.

On the way to Sunday Mass, she could clean and shine a station wagon loaded with seven children fresh from the farm. I often thought about her skills, but particularly so upon hearing of a giant oil spill in the Alaskan north some years ago. There was a problem with the cleanup and the news was not good. I thought if they would only send Mom there with a couple of packs of Kleenex, all would be clean and shiny in "two shakes of a Jiffy's tail."

In 1958, at age 67, Gramp shoveled seven-foot snowdrifts on a one-mile dirt farm road during an intense blizzard. He did that so Mom, his daughter, could depart for work.

Wherever I traveled, I simply had to put a nickel into a pay phone at 11:15 p.m. Eastern Standard Time and ask for an information operator in Newport, Rhode Island, and I would be connected with Mom immediately. That nickel expedited both nurturing and loving contact with her. It also meant that if she had forgotten to chastise me for something, she would not forgo the opportunity, with little regard for my circumstances at that point in time, where I happened to be, or what the true purpose of my call might have been.

I was on my bunk in a Southern Georgia army barracks, when the night guard entered and barked, "Kelly, your mother is on the phone!" I responded, "We don't have a phone in the barracks!" He growled, "She's on the pay phone outside, hurry up!" Even crusty sergeants responded to her power to intimidate and motivate over thousand of miles of phone lines.

She almost singlehandedly built the practice of our family physician, Doctor Bestoso. Mom was a game and willing participant in every type of test, procedure, surgery and recovery possibly known to medical science. Armed with a Blue Cross card and her unbending faith in Dr. Bestoso, the Blessed Virgin and Baby Jesus, Mom traversed the peaks and valleys of the marvelous mountain range of medical miracles, one by one.

Mom also had an ironclad method of judging a physician's ability. If the waiting room was packed and she had to wait an hour and a half to see the doctor, she would exclaim, "What a wonderful doctor he must be!"

The reward for her good judgment, journeys, waiting and commentary? She was healed of pervasive breast cancer in 1965 and its recurrence 30 years later, for one thing. Mom passed down a great lesson: We can be healed. The end result was always healing. Today, as we sit and worship before the God she so loved, her healing is complete.

Mom's father passed on her birthday, February 15th, so Mom obligingly passed on her father's birthday, May 12th, perhaps to complete the cycle.

She loved many people, places and things. Any child even remotely related to us or our friends was an automatic focal point of her love. As for people outside her domestic circle of nine and her extended family, she loved the Bishop, the Cardinal and His Holiness, the Pope. She worshiped God and prayed to Mary. We knelt together on many Monday nights and we prayed the novena when members of our family were in troubling circumstances: *Blessed be God. Blessed be His Holy Name. Blessed be Jesus Christ, true God and true man. Oh, Mary, conceived without sin, pray for us who have recourse to thee.*

Some things Mom loved were coffee cabinets, cube steak, a new car and the Irish Sweepstakes (a ticket was carefully placed beneath a statue of Mary at our home each year). She loved all puppies regardless of shape, size or breed. She loved the dog races in Taunton and she loved a steamed hot dog with mustard and a shake of celery salt. Some places Mom loved were New Hampshire, my brother Richard's restaurant, The Jack-O-Lantern resort and Roger Williams Park.

Today at dawn, I drove back to the farmland we once occupied. I'm sure Monet would have loved to be here with his easel.

Spring has kissed the land, caressed the meadows and sprinkled bright bows of blossoms upon the glen. True colors. Mom would love those colors because they revealed God's beauty, grace and love. Subtle greens, lovely pinks, rich lavenders, bright yellow streams of sunshine trimming sunlit, teal pastures. Could Heaven be more glorious? I do think so!

The hen coops have been replaced by stylish residences. Our front step is gone. Others now inhabit the hills of home. Those we knew there are no longer present. Those we yearn to speak with again, for just a fleeting moment, are now somewhere else. People we knew and loved are far away, their voices long ago silenced by time, toil and the toll of life.

Mother, oh Mother! Today I see your "True Colors" shining through like a rainbow on a spring morning. I see them shining through and they're beautiful.

I often tell my estate-planning clients to take plenty of time to pat each other on the back as they go through the planning process. Most of their lifelong efforts have actually been for the benefit of others.

Most of the lifelong efforts of Mom, Dad and Gramp were for our benefit, and so I would like to say this to them today, as they are reunited in Heaven:

As you look down upon those you created, those warmly welcomed into your lives, those you loved and who loved you, and those whose lives you touched, I have an idea...

Mom, Dad and Gramp, today in Heaven take time out to congratulate and hug each other. Take time out to give yourselves a very big pat on the back.

CHAPTER TWENTY-NINE
The Day I Live

The day I live is going to be really great! I will visit the folks, pet the dog, take all the kids out for ice cream in a large station wagon and let their mom sleep in. I'll mow the lawn, take a nap and walk on the beach. The water will be clear, but there will be a playful surf. The nap will be short but invigorating. The mowed grass will smell fresh and somewhat sweet. I'll return with some green, some black and some blue from each event on the day I live.

The day I live will be different from all other days I spend, waiting for the day I live. Those days are not practice days; they are more like prison. I am waiting for the day I live and I know it is coming. The day I live will be so glorious that I'll forget all this pain. I'll be famous on the day I live. Some people will stop me on the street to shake my hand. Others will just want to chat with me. I will walk down Main Street, eat some apple pie and autograph copies of my book. I won't strut, but I just might saunter, as I walk down Main.

Eventually, the sun will set on the day I live and I will head for home. People there will yell at me, telling me I'm not good enough and calling me a phony. They will make fun of me and say I don't care enough. They will call me a liar and a cheat. People there have power over me. They will not believe there was a day when I lived, or if they do, they will joke about it. Yet

I will know I was famous on that day, because on the day I lived, people loved me and I made a difference.

The day I lived is now just a memory. The people who loved me are fading from view. The people who journeyed with me are getting old and gray. There is little hope to live one more day. My existence is a prison and I am thirsting for the day I die.

On the day I die, I hope I can remember the day I lived. I hope I can remember to be thankful for that one day and for all those handshakes and smiles and blessings. Maybe that's all life grants us. A day to live. A day of perfection. A wedding, a christening, a graduation, a funeral. One perfect day per life to live. Will you know it when it arrives, dear reader?